Balls, Gloves

The Sporting Legacy of the Chisnall Brothers in Rugby League and Boxing

Eric Chisnall and Andrew Quirke

Vertical Editions

www.verticaleditions.com

First published in the United Kingdom in 2013 by Vertical
Editions, Unit 4a, Snaygill Industrial Estate, Skipton, North
Yorkshire BD23 2QR

www.verticaleditions.com

ISBN 978-1-904091-71-4

A CIP catalogue record for this book is available from the
British Library

Cover design by HBA, York

Printed and bound by MPG, Bodmin

This book is dedicated to my parents, my wife Elaine, my children and my brothers for all their love and support.

I would also like to thank everyone who gave of their time to help with this book.

Eric Chisnall

*****

My work on this book is dedicated with all my love to my son, Oliver.

Andrew Quirke

Contents

Contents

Acknowledgements

The book you are holding in your hands cannot solely be attributed to my efforts. There have been huge contributions and kind offers of assistance that have made this project a reality. That being the case, there are a number of people I'd like to thank in no particular order.

First of all, many thanks to the staff and players at **St Helens RLFC** who were absolutely fantastic in their assistance with this project. Their involvement just demonstrates the esteem in which Eric is held at the club as a common phrase I heard was 'I'll do anything for Chissy'. A big thanks to **Steve Leonard** at Saints for approaching me to ask me to work on the book and thanks to **Neil Kilshaw** for recommending me. Huge thanks as ever to **Mike Appleton**, the fantastic media manager at Saints. As many supporters will tell you, nothing is ever too much trouble for Mike and he is an absolute credit to the club. With this and other projects, Mike has always been incredibly helpful. For this book, he helped me gain access to members of the first team squad for interviews as well as kindly allowing me behind the scenes at Langtree Park to take the photo of the superb Chisnall mural honouring both Eric and Dave.

Massive thanks to **Mike Rush** and his team including **Derek Traynor** and others for very kindly allowing me open access to Saints' state of the art training facility at Cowley. They went above and beyond allowing me to interview under 20s players who had previously gone on Australian tours with Eric as well as allowing me to photograph Eric putting the under 18s side through their paces. My only problem was that it was on the coldest January night possible and I've only just regained the feeling in my fingers. Thanks to **the players** there who took time out of training to give me their memories of Eric. Mike leads a fantastic team at Cowley including **Paul Molyneux** who also arranged for me to have copies of the great Australian Academy tour photos to use in this book. I also have to thank **Paul Clough, Jonny Lomax** and **James Roby** for their interviews. Big thanks to **James Graham** for very kindly emailing me from Australia.

Many thanks to **Tom Van Vollenhoven** for agreeing to write the foreword for this book and **Mike Donnison** for making it possible.

Thanks to **Gary Connolly** for taking time out on a Saturday to come and speak to me in St Helens.

Big thanks to **Alex Murphy** who I have interviewed for a number of my books now and is always giving of his time and memories.

Thanks also to **Ken Kelly** who took time out to speak to me and gave me great memories of his friendship with Dave.

Thanks to **Don Joy** and **Phillipa Ivory** at the **New Zealand Rugby League** for putting me in contact with **Mike McClennan** and big thanks to Mike himself for making contact with me over the phone.

Big thanks to **Mike Critchley** whose help was invaluable on the research side of things. His memories, particularly in regards to Dave's career, were so detailed it really helped shape the sections of the book covering Dave. Mike encouraged me to take a step out of my comfort zone with this book. Although it is my 10th release, it is the first I have done as a biography rather than a 'ghosted' autobiography. The thought scared me at first but it has meant for a better book. He is also another person who is always happy to provide useful contacts. That brings me nicely to **Andy Wilson, Neil Barraclough** and **Phil Wilkinson**, all of whom provided contacts for this book. Thanks to **'lambretta'** on the Leigh Centurions message board for the statistics on Les's Leigh career. Many thanks to **Danny** and **John Butler** who kindly lent me DVDs of the 1974 Ashes series and to **Brian Peers** for the photo of Eric receiving the Ward Trophy on the front cover.

Thanks go out to **Alex Service** who kindly allowed me the use of text he had put together for a 'this is your life' style brochure on Eric.

A huge thanks to **Karl Waddicor** of **Vertical Editions** for his work on making this book a reality.

I'd also like to thank **Louise Woodward-Styles** for her help with the title and invaluable marketing skills.

I am very fortunate that because of my previous Rugby League related books, I can generally get hold of most personalities within the game for interviews. That also shows how much that Rugby League really is a family with players always willing to help each other. As this book focuses on all four Chisnall brothers, that meant I was entering into a new sport, as John was a professional boxer turned boxing coach. As much as I enjoy watching boxing, I had no contacts within the sport and feared it would be a very tight knit community to try and get into. So, I have to give massive thanks to top boxer **Martin Murray**. Not only is Martin a genuinely top man who allowed me to interview him during preparations for his 2011 world title fight against Felix Sturm but he regularly texted me with numerous contacts to interview about John. I can't thank Martin enough for him opening many doors for me in the sport. A shout of thanks to **Sadie Sherran** for putting me in touch with Martin in the first place too.

One of the people Martin introduced me to was a member of his family, **Buller Greenhalgh**. His recollections of John's early life were invaluable.

A big thanks to **Paul Spink** of **Brand Hatton** for helping me set up the interview with **Craig Lyon**. My apologies to Craig for waking him up with my phone call!

A huge amount of appreciation goes to **Wynford Jones**

of the **British Boxing Board of Control** for his fantastic work in providing me with the details of John's professional boxing career including John's original boxing application.

Thanks to **Gary Davies** for his interviews where he provided great memories of John.

Same goes for **Tony Clarey** whose interview showed a humorous side to John too.

Big thanks also to **Sean Casey** for his personal insight into growing up with the Chisnalls as his uncles.

Many thanks to **Lowe House Boxing club** too for allowing me to take photographs of their tribute to John.

Practicalities now and I have to say thanks to my mate **Paul Gill**, without whom I wouldn't have had a chance of physically committing this book to computer. My previous laptop died in pretty spectacular fashion and Paul very kindly allowed me use of a laptop and said there was no rush giving it back. Thanks to that offer, I was able to get this book written. He also keeps my feet on the ground by calling me 'bighead' after my book plugging on Facebook. Thanks also to **Rob Barton**, whose IT skills allowed me to retrieve work I previously thought had been lost in the aforementioned laptop meltdown.

Big thanks to **Fiee Shiel** for providing me with the loan of her camera for use at Saints' training session. Also thanks for the best laugh of 2011 which involved a stack of mini pizzas.

Thanks to **Chris Fray** who brought to my attention the quote from Mary Anne Radmacher that I've used at the end of the book.

A massive thank you to **Dani Moore** who is very supportive of my book projects. It damns her with faint praise if I said she proofed this book as it was much more than that with Dani suggesting improvements, changes in ordering of sections and rewording sections. All from someone who isn't a Rugby League fan too. You are a star

Dani and I can't thank you enough for your help when you already had huge commitments outside work.

Some personal thanks now if you'd bear with me, again in no particular order …

My **mum** for her ongoing support.

Kate Wilkinson who is always very supportive of my book projects and understands what my word count posts on Facebook are all about.

A big thanks to **Tamsyn Haselden** who really made my night by supporting the book launch of the **Graeme West** project. Sticking with Graeme, I'd like to thank him for being such a great guy to work alongside and his funny anecdote about Dave for this book. Big thanks for exactly the same reasons to **Paul Loughlin**, another champion fella who also provided memories for this book.

Personal thanks to **Gail Yates, Caron Campbell, Graham Wilson, Ben Smithurst, Richard Luck, Niccy Shiel, Ian Penketh** and **Ste Radford** for general support and encouragement.

Big thanks to **Michelle Dudley** who kindly offered her services as sounding board on this project and generally gave great advice throughout.

Thanks to **Chris Gill** and **Mike Gill** for their ongoing support and encouragement as always.

Special mention to the two people I text and ring probably more than anybody else in relation to the progress of my book projects and they are **Paul Bennett** and **Kev Gill**. Always incredibly supportive of my books and always willing to lend an ear to my ideas and damn good friends.

Finally and most importantly, I want to thank the **Chisnall family** for allowing me into their lives to tell their fascinating story. **Eric**, who I made contact with first, put up with my hours of questions with great patience and welcomed me into his home. It's been a pleasure to spend time with such a legend of the club that I support. Eric's modesty at his own great achievements meant that he wanted the spotlight to shine across all four Chisnall men in this book. **Dave** also kindly welcomed me into his home and told his story with great humour and emotion, a genuinely lovely man. **Les** also welcomed me into his home and was giving of his memories, for which I am very grateful. **John,** of course, is sadly no longer with us so I never got to meet him in person. Through the passion and love of the recollections of his fighters, friends and fellow trainers though I feel like I do know him. I hope this has translated to this book and that I have done him justice.

It was a big responsibility and challenge telling four people's stories in one book. The reputation of the Chisnall family speaks for itself, their achievements in their own sporting careers were huge and their contribution to the legacy of sport going forward is assured through the stars they have helped to create and the young lives they have positively influenced.

Andrew J Quirke

Life is for livin'
Andrew J Quirke

Foreword

I was nearing the end of my St Helens career when the club drew against Warrington in the 1967 Lancashire Cup Final. The replay was scheduled for Station Road, Swinton and I felt we needed something different for the game.

That being the case, I approached our coach at the time Joe Coan to suggest he pick young forward, Eric Chisnall, who had impressed me in his performances at the start of his career.

Fortunately, Joe agreed with me and Eric took the opportunity with both hands. He scored the match winning try in that game and he never looked back. I had enjoyed many glorious years at St Helens, a club I loved and it was great to see a young local lad start out on a long successful career of his own. I felt the club would be in good hands as I retired.

Eric would go on to become a giant of the St Helens club, playing more than 500 times for the side, lifting numerous trophies and earning deserved England and Great Britain caps.

I learnt though that there was far more to the Chisnall family than Eric.

There was Les, a talented centre who became the first of the family to lift the great Challenge Cup with Leigh at Wembley in 1971.

Then there was the much travelled Dave, a fearsome warrior of a prop forward, equally adept at throwing a punch as throwing a dummy. In 1970 he became the youngest ever prop forward to tour Australia with Great Britain, a true measure of how tough a player he was. What a character too!

Finally, there was eldest brother John who was a

professional boxer turned trainer. Whilst John has sadly departed, his boxing, training and developing of young talent sees his name well and truly live on.

Four remarkable sporting careers all ably forged by being brought up in tough times by their mum Alice.

I returned to St Helens recently to officially open their magnificent new Langtree Park stadium and there stood as part of the guard of honour with a typically big smile was Eric. I know with him still being involved in junior development at the club, the flow of young talent that is the lifeblood of Saints will fill the great stadium with great players for a long time to come.

I know Eric will instil the Saints players of the future with the same principles I had as a player: determination, never cutting corners and belief.

The legacy of the Chisnall family lives on through players they have helped shape such as James Roby, Jonny Lomax and James Graham or boxers like Martin Murray.

Now their story, of four brothers, is finally written down in this book, it will be part of their legacy too.

This book details the hardships and triumphs on and off the field that the four men have experienced; the family that played together has stayed together.

I hope you enjoy the stories that this biography tells, and which all play a part in showing that not only were the Chisnalls great sportsmen but they are great people too.

Tom Van Vollenhoven

1

Havelock Street

On the face of it, Havelock Street in the 1940s was just another row of terraced houses in the town of St Helens. A town economically depressed during an era of general financial hardship. Yet, one of the small houses on this ordinary street was home to a family that was anything but ordinary.

Alice and Tom Chisnall had seven children; three girls (Edie, Lily and Audrey) and four boys. The eldest son, John was followed by Les then in July 1946 Eric and last but not least, the baby of the family Dave in April 1948.

Eric remembers, 'We got on well as kids most of the time. At the younger end of the family, there were only two years between me, Les and Dave. Then one of my sisters was seven years older.'

Although times were hard, Eric recalls a real sense of community: 'It was a marvellous community around that area, everybody knew one another. There was no trouble and you could keep your door open at night. In the summer months, we could play out until it went dark at ten o clock. We'd get called in then and would have to head home but people weren't frightened of letting kids out in those days. Everybody just mucked in and helped one another. That was the society that we lived in.'

Dad Tom had played Rugby League for a number of local sides as Eric details: 'My dad had played a little bit of rugby for the Golden Lion and then Wigan Highfield as well as one of the many amateur sides in St Helens of the time, Vine Tavern. They would take on intriguingly named opponents such as Unos Dabs. They used to call him 'ferret' as he was only slim whilst my mother was a big woman. We were all big kids with our John being the smallest and perhaps the toughest too!'

Dave recalls: 'Dad was only little, around five foot six; he played scrum half. He was only around ten stone.'

Tragedy befell the family when Tom died at an early age. Les describes the memory, 'My first real memory is of my dad dying when I was eight, somebody told me at school. It happened when he was walking across some waste ground. He was around 53 when he died.' Eric recalls, 'The only thing I remember about it was that in those days they would lay the deceased out in the downstairs front room. Somebody lifted me up to look at him and that moment stuck with me for the rest of my life. I never saw another dead body until my wife's father died many years later.'

As well as the devastating emotional loss, without the main breadwinner, the family's financial hardship increased. Eric remembers the situation: 'It was a bit of a tough upbringing because my dad died when I was six and our Dave was only four. It was hard going. They were tough times and my mother brought us up, me, my three sisters and my three brothers. My eldest brother and eldest sister both found partners and got married. My second eldest sister never got married so she helped to contribute to the upbringing of us. Her wages were a big help and added to the benefits the family received which I don't think were a great deal back in those days. Everybody was struggling but I do remember times when we would get a cheque and would be able to buy a pair of shoes or a pair of pants. That would happen once every 12 months and would help keep us going. Once our shoes wore out, we would have to put a bit of cardboard in the bottom of them to keep them going. That was okay until it started raining and then they would get a bit soggy. Me, Les and Dave would have one pair of rugby boots between the three of us. First up best dressed was very much the order of the day.

'Lil's wage packet and my mam's widow's pension were all we had to keep the family going. Back then, people used to say it was degrading for some children to receive free school dinners, I was just glad to be getting food. From an early age, I realised that I had to do something with my life and would have to buckle down. It was hard times but we were and remain a close knit family which helped us get through. We were just lucky that the three of us were good at rugby. We've all done okay out of it.'

Les agrees: 'It was hard for all of us in that house, especially heating wise. During the winter, it was really cold. We used to knot papers together if we could find any with old lino or old shoes when we weren't wearing them. We always got second hand clothes from a place in Peter Street or hand me downs from somebody else.'

Dave points out although they were difficult days, mum Alice was the driving force of the family. 'It was rough round Havelock Street. There were the four boys and Edie, Lily and Audrey, seven of us with our mum. That was in a two bedroom terraced house. My mum lost two kids as well. They weren't brilliant days.

'My mum looked after us. Nobody dared touch us. I think having it tough growing up meant we all appreciated it later on when we got things. When my dad died when I was four, we had nothing. We had a very good mother though.'

Family friend Buller Greenhalgh recalls Alice: 'She used to organise spud picking. It was a hard life for the mum. She was a big woman and she kept the family together.'

Eric recalls her formidable reputation: 'My mum, Alice,

was a well known woman around the Havelock Street area. She was the salt of the earth and the things she used to do were unbelievable. She used to look after us; if one of us misbehaved she would give us a clip round the ear hole. The other way, if someone had a go at us and we'd done nothing wrong she would stick up for us and defend us. There weren't many people who crossed her. She was a good woman. If anybody in our street died, she would go across and lay out the deceased for the undertaker which would save the bereaved family some money. She would also go round and collect for flowers for the funeral.

'We all went to St Thomas's school in Peter Street and then we all went on to St Mary's. I think it was the same headmaster for all of us through all that time: Mr Skidmore. My mum had a few skirmishes with him when she felt any of the teachers were treating us unfairly. So my mum was well known there as well!'

Whilst the Chisnall men agree on their upbringing, some understandable differences in opinion appear when discussing which brother picked on which.

Les's view is: 'Eric used to pick on all of us, he was wild. That might surprise people as we all come across as quite laid back these days.'

Dave is even more forthright: 'I was the youngest of the family so I did have to fight for everything. Eric used to knock lumps out of me. I used to try and hang about with him. I got him back when I played against him later on though. I used to get laid on every day at home by Eric and Les. If I said the wrong thing I would get a dig'. This did benefit Dave though as he admits: 'Nobody put on me because I had grown up with three older brothers. One ended up a professional boxer and the other two were rugby players.'

Eric recalls a closeness with younger brother Dave: 'With Dave being the youngest of the family and me the second youngest, we used to be together most of the time growing

19

up.'

What was clear was that when the boys went to school, St Thomas's and then later St Mary's, each had to fight their own battles. Eric explains: 'We all learnt to be able to look after ourselves at school if there was bother. Our Les had been at school two years before I went but if I got into any trouble, he would tell me to sort it myself unless it was somebody older. You had to be able to stand on your own two feet, if you caused trouble you had to be the one to get yourself out of it. It made sure I didn't get too big headed and start causing trouble knowing I had an older brother who could sort it out for me.

'I was pretty well behaved at school, I suppose my one regret would be in those days, people just wanted to finish school and get a job. I did the same myself and I regret that looking back. I tell my grandkids today that the best thing that they can have is an education. Money can't buy you an education; it's the best thing for you.'

Dave was also keen to leave his school days behind him: 'I played both football and rugby for the school but I never liked school. I couldn't wait to get away from it as I wasn't a very good learner. All the others in the family were. I never used to be able to take it all in.'

Outside of school, the boys quickly grew a love of sport, typically for St Helens; this generally took the form of street games of Rugby League. Les remembers: 'I never played rugby at school because St Mary's didn't have a team at the time. We played once at Bishop Road and the teacher put me forward for some trials at Rivington Road. There was that much competition when I got there that I don't think I got a pass.

'Most of my rugby was played in the streets at that age. We used to have some good times rugby wise. We would go to the park if we could get a ball.'

Eric adds: 'We would play football out on the streets

and when summer came we would get wickets out and accidentally smash the odd window! As soon as the ball would go through a pane of glass, we would all disappear back into our house whilst the aggrieved home owner would come looking for us.

'We would also go to Rec Park and play sport for hours on end. We would stand in a line whilst teams would get picked and you could easily tell if you were any good or not. If you always got left last to be picked, you were hopeless. You just moved up the ladder a bit until you were first to be picked.

'Neither St Thomas's nor St Mary's were rugby schools so we had never really played rugby. In my last year at St Thomas's, former Saints player Don Gullick turned up. He took us for a few games amongst ourselves but at least we were playing a bit of rugby. At St Mary's, it was mainly football. I used to play for the school team there in the year above. I also played cricket for the school team. I always loved rugby though and we used to play that when we were at home. There were plenty of good players in the area where we lived.'

The boys' heroes growing up could all be found on a Saturday afternoon playing Rugby League at Knowsley Road for the famous St Helens club and the Chisnall family were regular visitors to the stadium.

Eric would go to great lengths to watch a match: 'I used to go watching Saints when I could afford it. Most of the time I couldn't afford it and would go up Borough Road, under the tunnels, through the gas and lecky, down the railway line then over the wall of the ground without paying. Now and again it would be that bad a game that when we tried to climb back out they'd make us go back in!

'There used to be a chap who would pedal his tricycle up to Knowsley Road on match day. The three of us would wait for him at Wilson Street and push him up to Saints on a

Saturday afternoon. It got us in for nothing. He used to have to find his own way home though.'

Once inside, the importance of the Saints players to the young Chisnall boys was clear as Dave recalls: 'I feel that supporters today don't really think back to days gone by. When we were young, that's what we were built on. I was a Saints fan growing up. I used to go and sit on the wall at Knowsley Road and watch them. It was amazing watching the likes of Vinty Karalius, Vollenhoven and Murphy. They were heroes to me.'

Although money was scarce for the family, St Helens making the Challenge Cup Final of 1956 meant that somehow, they would be making the trip down to Wembley. Again, mum Alice was the driving force as Eric remembers: 'My first big Saints memory was them getting to Wembley in 1956. It was against Halifax. She got us on a coach to Wembley which left Havelock Street at midnight. We got into London about seven o' clock in the morning. That left us with about five hours of walking around. We were the first in the stadium. We were right on the wall and nobody could block our view. It was a magnificent stadium. It was the 28th of April, 1956 which was my mum's birthday. We had a really good time. It was the first time Saints won the Challenge Cup so it was an amazing occasion. I went back to watch Saints win there in '61 and '66, played for them on the winning side in '72 and '76 so in my first five visits, we didn't lose.'

Whilst future Wembley appearances were at this stage just a dream, three of the Chisnall brothers would indeed go on to achieve that goal. The eldest, John, had given Rugby League a try but his career soon went in another direction. Eric explains: 'Our John played a little bit of Rugby League as well. He was quite decent at it but he was more into the boxing. John had always been into boxing as my dad had been big on it. My dad would take John to Britannia Boxing

Club at Peasley Cross as well as Lowe House Boxing Club. There were a few boxers in our street such as Freddy Groves. There were a lot of tough nuts in Havelock Street. Nobody would mess with them.'

Les remembers his dad's keen interest in John's boxing too, 'I went to watch John box once as an amateur at Lowe House club. My dad was with him, I remember him talking to him and rubbing him down afterwards. My dad really looked after him.'

Buller Greenhalgh, John's best friend, and grandfather of top boxer Martin Murray, takes up the story: 'I knew John all my life. We lived across the road from each other. There was only about nine months' difference in age between us.

'We would work on the St Helens markets on a Saturday. I was on the lino stall, John on the fruit stall. We used to knock about and had the odd fall out as lads do.

'John started in boxing when Harry Cain used to take us in a room above his shop near Napier Street. We would train there, he only had one bag. That's where most of the boxers in the area started out. John was a fair boxer.'

John and Buller, whilst still only young, worked down the pit and both suffered injuries. Buller explains: 'We worked down the pit for a couple of years. What happened to him though is that he got hurt down the pit when he was about 16 or 17. He had injured his back. I got hurt myself in a separate incident. He was off work for a good while and was in convalescence for an equally long time. He would go to Oakmere Hall in Sandiway near Northwich. He would go on a Monday for his rehabilitation and come home Friday.'

Whilst his back injury would continue to give John problems for many years, his determination meant that even wearing a crate strapped to his back for some time would not stop him doing what he loved: boxing. Buller reveals the lengths John would go to for competition: 'They used to have a boxing show at the fair. The man running it would get somebody up on stage and get them to hold a matchbox in his hand which he would chop in half with a sword. John was always mad keen to get on that stage. They would also have last man standing boxing at those fairs too. You would get 5 bob or 25p for winning and it was vicious. He wouldn't back down from anything. He would have a go at anybody.'

2

The Rise of 'Johnny James'

John had been working as a steel erector whilst continuing with his amateur boxing career. He had married early in life and moved away from the family home in Havelock Street to Peasley Cross.

Eric remembers: 'John had a tremendous amateur boxing record, when my dad died they wanted him to turn professional but he couldn't because he was the breadwinner for the rest of us first then for his own family when he got married.'

Subsequently, John only turned professional in 1963 where his application for a boxing licence reveals he fought under the name 'Johnny James'. Eric remembers: 'John had left it too late in life and I don't think he was the fittest at the time. It was a meal ticket. He fought at light heavyweight and he was only really a middleweight. If he could have made the weight at middleweight, he would have done some damage.'

John fought professionally eight times. His first fight was in October 1963 and was a win over Bernie Sutton at the Free Trade Hall, Manchester. The next month on the 19th November he faced and defeated Colin Woodman at the grandly named Majestic Ballroom in Finsbury Park. Just six days later, John fought again, beating Dave Brodie by disqualification at Kings Hall, Belle Vue.

At the turn of 1964, John gained his fourth professional

victory with a third round knockout of Johnny Plenty at the National Sporting Club, London.

It is perhaps John's fifth professional bout that was his most notable. He took on Jack London Junior at Tower Circus, Blackpool; his family was in support that evening.

Eric remembers: 'John got disqualified against Jack London for hitting him when he was already heading towards the canvas. London was already on the way down and John just thought he would make doubly sure. According to form, London said John shouldn't have been disqualified as he would have done the same thing.'

Les recalls: 'I don't think our John should have been disqualified as Jack wasn't really down when John hit him again. Brian London said, "Who the hell's put our Jack in with him?" Our John had really battered him.'

The disqualification loss would be followed by three further bouts, all resulting in knock out defeats to John. There was no shame in this though as a 4th May defeat was to 'Young' John McCormack who went on to become British Light Heavyweight Champion.

His final fight was on 26th November, 1964 against Roy Seward, and again his brothers were there.

Eric reflects on John's professional career: 'He wouldn't back down from anything and that was just what was in him. I think my dad made him that way. My dad was only a little fella but was as tough as they come. You had to be tough in those days and fight for everything in life.'

John was a top notch amateur boxer and had taken some impressive fights in his professional career. Boxing could be lonely, after all, once the bell rings, fighters are in the ring on their own with no teammates to dig them out of a hole. Couple that with the rigorous training requirements and John's achievements as a fighter reflected against the family's tough upbringing were no mean feat. Although his career as a boxer was over, his impact on the sport would actually increase in later years.

His burgeoning training techniques hinted at the future, Dave recalls: 'When I first started playing rugby, John would give me training. Boxing training, I believe, is the best training that you will ever get. All rugby players are hitting bags these days.'

Second oldest brother Les also had designs on a professional career but his sights were set on only one target: to play professional rugby league for St Helens. 'I worked for Greenall Whitley, I was third man with Ken Leyland. When we had spare time, we would throw a ball round in the cab. Ken asked if I fancied playing. I said that I would give it a go. I had a fair bit of knowledge on how to play rugby from playing in the streets. I was only 16 at this point but he got in touch with Albert Butler who was running the A and B teams at Saints. He got me a couple of trials up there.

'I watched the legendary Len Killeen train whilst at Saints and got to play alongside Keith Northey.

'I had one game in the A team against Rochdale and I played in the B team at Clock Face. I didn't have any training gear so I never went again. I had no boots or anything. I bumped into Albert Butler some time after and he told me that I shouldn't have worried about that as they would have sorted me out somehow. I had nobody to guide me along, no father. Even though my mam did a great job looking after us, you sometimes need that father figure to push you a little bit.'

With that twist of fate regarding the training gear, Les missed out on the opportunity to play professionally for Saints. His new target was to play for another club.

He remembers: 'I then had trials at Leigh, but I only had the two games. Oldham were advertising for players so I wrote to them. I never had a game with them though. Geoff Fletcher used to pick me up but it was difficult to finish work then get back for Geoff to pick me up outside the White Hart pub to take me to Oldham. I got a bit sick of that. Work wasn't a case of clock on and clock off, I could only leave when all the work was done.'

With work and travel difficulties putting paid to any chance of a career at Oldham, Les concentrated on playing amateur rugby league in far less grand surroundings than Knowsley Road.

'A chap at Greenalls was getting a team together at Rainhill Ex Servicemen's and they were struggling for players. He asked me if I fancied coming and I said yes. There were no cars then so I had to get the number 7 bus from town. I then had to walk from Rainhill bridge right down towards Rainhill Stoops. I had a few games there which I enjoyed. We had no changing rooms so built a shed to get changed in. We would wash in a puddle if it was raining. Then it was back on the bus to get home again.'

So keen was Les on his rugby for the Ex Servicemen's he also helped the club in other ways: 'I used to go down on a Saturday morning to mark the pitch out. I was 18 then. We were playing Beechams. In the game I scored under the sticks and my sister's husband Joe Casey was refereeing and he disallowed the try. I asked him, "why?" and he explained that there was no dead ball line so I must have gone dead. I told him, "thanks a lot." 'I had forgotten to mark out the dead ball line.'

Where Les led, Eric and Dave would soon follow. Eric recalls: 'Les said to me one Saturday that they were a bit stuck for players and did I fancy having a game. I went up and played for them. That was how it all started for me. When I went to Rainhill Ex Servicemen's I was told that Saints wanted to see me and Terry Cross. I thought somebody was taking the mickey out of me. I refused to believe them and didn't go to Knowsley Road. Saints had signed players from there before but I hadn't been playing long and didn't think it could be true.'

A couple of weeks later Dave came up and started playing for them too despite his tender age. 'He was a bit of a fiery sod, our Dave and he never took a backward step.'

'We played against Blackbrook. Old Harold Swift was playing on the wing for them. Dave came across and shoulder charged him, sending him about 10 feet in the air. Harold ended up flat on his back.'

Eric soon took to playing the game for the Ex Servicemen but injury threatened a very promising career. 'After about seven games, we faced the famous St Helens club, Pilkington Recs. I got tackled and ended up breaking my wrist. I went to the Providence Hospital to see the locally famous Sister Duffy who everybody used to go to.

'A man who had followed us to the hospital, turned out to be a scout for Leigh. He told me that he wanted me and Les to come to Leigh. I told him that I had broken my wrist but he insisted he wanted me to go down and see Gerry Helme. On the Tuesday, he took us down there even though my arm was in plaster and a sling. He told me to come down again when I was fit but I wasn't interested. If I was going to play for anybody, it was only going to be Saints.

'I soon got to know Sister Duffy after I broke my wrist. One of Wilf Smith's sayings in those days if you gave a daft pass out was that it was a "Sister Duffy pass". She was notorious and never seemed to have any sympathy for any of her patients. She used to treat everybody the same and she was one on her own. I did my collarbone at Rochdale when I first signed for Saints. I used to go the 'Provi' and had it treated by having a figure eight shaped device around each shoulder. Your shoulders would be pulled back, and after about three or four weeks it would start to relax and you would think "thank God for that". 'Then Sister Duffy would start tying it back again until I could hardly breathe. She had to do it three or four times before it was healed.'

Sadly, the Ex Servicemen's team disbanded and many of the players went to play for Pilkingtons Recs including the Chisnall brothers. Les stayed at Recs the longest – four years – enjoying his stint at the club in the centre position. Eric was settling into the second row whilst burly Dave was already a formidable prop forward. However, the younger two brothers weren't destined to stay in the amateur ranks for very long.

3

Turning Professional

St Helens had beaten old rivals Wigan in the 1966 Challenge Cup Final. The all-conquering team of '66 is still spoken of in hushed tones by Saints supporters with long memories. The cup triumph capped off a remarkable season for the club as they had also captured the Championship, Leaders Shield and Lancashire League trophies. However, it also heralded a dramatic episode featuring one of the club's favourite sons. Eric remembers: 'After Wembley in 1966, Alex Murphy didn't go back to Saints; he was in dispute with the club all that year. Saints were struggling for centres at the time, they bought Tommy Bishop and had him and Peter Harvey as the halves and in their wisdom, moved Murphy out to centre. Alex didn't like it. He ended up going to Leigh as player coach. Alex was such a good player that wherever you put him, he would be the best player on the field. He later played scrum half for both Leigh and Warrington and took both teams to Wembley. There's been some really good players in Rugby League; the likes of Roger Millward then Hardisty and Hepworth at Leeds.

'In my opinion, Alex Murphy was the best player ever to play the game of Rugby League. You can watch video of him when he was on a Lions tour at just 18 years of age. He just tore the Aussies to shreds and he was like lightning from a standing start. He had the all round game. He had a kicking game, defensively he was really good. Don't forget, he got rules changed in the game. He was putting over so many drop goals, they devalued them. When we played Wigan at Wembley in 1966, Wigan had no recognised hooker whereas we had Bill Sayer who we had signed from Wigan. What used to happen in the game then was if you went offside, there would be a kick to touch followed by a scrum. Of course, Saints were winning the ball in every scrum. Every time Wigan got the ball that day, Alex just went and stood offside. They changed the rules after that.'

As for Eric himself: 'I started playing for Pilks Recs. I had only played about three or four games. I was working in the gas works at the time. We were in the cabin and someone said to a colleague, "You're something to do with scouting at Wigan aren't you? Well Eric plays rugby". That's all that was said but he took my name and I never thought any more about it. A week or so later, an old man turned up at our house but I was working that day. He walked from our house to the gas works to see me. He told me he had been to see me play at Warrington for Pilks and he wanted me to come and have trials at Wigan. I went and had trials. I would get the bus to Haresfinch where I would meet Johnny Jackson and another St Helens lad, Dennis Murphy. Dennis had been a really good scrum half as a schoolboy but never went much further. Johnny went on to play for the Wigan first team. I played a couple of trials, the first one being Rochdale away.

'They had some characters then. They had a powerful Fijian playing for them and a prop called Kettleton. I tackled this Kettleton and as I did so, he bit the top of my arm. I gave him a right mouthful and he replied: "If you tackle me again, I'll bite your other arm". 'He was notorious in the game at the time. Things changed for me a little bit after my second trial match for Wigan. Basil Lowe from Saints came to our house and told me he wanted me to go and see Mr. Cook (the legendary chairman Harry Cook) at Forest

Grove up in Eccleston Park. They'd been given my name by Mitchells Ice Cream who'd told Len Kilshaw it was terrible that a St Helens lad had to go and have trials at Wigan. They sent the scout, Johnny King, to watch me while I was playing for Wigan 'A'. Mr. Cook said: "Look, we've been watching you, you've got one match left to play but I will tell you, anything Wigan offer you we will give you more". I had a lad who was looking after me at the time called Billy Shiels. We didn't really know much about negotiations so just asked for £1,000, £400 straight away followed by another £600 after 10 first team appearances. I played my last game, and had a meeting with Wigan where I told them I didn't really want to sign for what they were offering. I immediately signed for Saints on the 22nd December 1966.'

Eric was now a Saint however it had nearly not been the case and the minutes of the St Helens club for 22nd November 1966 showed that the club themselves thought the opportunity might well have been lost: 'It was reported that this player (Chisnall) had been contacted but had already signed for trials with Wigan'.

The late George Parsons, a former Saints' second-rower was chairman of Pilkington Recs in 1966 and talked about his involvement with the Eric Chisnall saga and the old enemy: 'One particularly pleasing aspect was seeing Eric Chisnall become a big name at Saints – he's in their Hall of Fame now – but I remember getting a telling off when he was attracting attention at the Recs! There was this fellow on the touchline and I asked him who he was. Apparently he was a Wigan scout, who said he was looking to see who the best players were to recommend to the Central Park club. I said: "What if a player, who might be the best prospect, has an off-day? I'll tell you who I think the best player is if you ask me!" Anyhow, he took our second-rower, Eric Chisnall, for trials. Meanwhile, I got a telephone call from someone at Saints who sounded quite upset. "Have you lost your loyalty to Saints? You've got a good player there and you let him go to Wigan!" I said that I didn't tell Eric where to go, but Wigan had made him an offer and if St Helens improved it, he would probably end up at Knowsley Road, which of course, he did in the end. Eric was a good player for us, as was his brother Les who played in the centre.'

Eric's signing for the Knowsley Road club was listed in the minutes of the St Helens Board for 22nd December as follows: 'The chairman reported that Eric Chisnall had been signed at a total fee of £1,000, this to be paid £400 on signing, with a further £600 after 10 first team matches. The action taken by the chairman was approved by the board as was a payment of £20 to W. Shiels for his assistance in the signing.'

As to what it meant to Eric: 'It's hard to describe what signing for Saints meant to me. It's difficult to put into words how it feels to do something you've always really wanted to do. I'd been watching the likes of Van Vollenhoven, Murphy, Watson, Warlow, Sayer and Mantle. Then there was Halsall, Benyon and Frankie Barrow. They were all great, great players. It was so, so good. My mum was delighted as you can imagine. If I'd have signed for Wigan, she would have disowned me. She was just St Helens through and through.'

Signing for Saints wasn't the end of the journey though, merely the first steps in a much bigger adventure, the first stages of which were practicalities like getting his kit.

'Just at the top end of Havelock Street was Jackie Pimblett who had just signed for Saints; his dad had previously played for Belle Vue. He was winding me up a little although I didn't know it at the time. He advised me that when I went to my first training session, I wouldn't need to take any training gear or boots. He said I would be given all new training gear when I arrived at the club. I came down the famous old tunnel rather sheepishly and as I was going in, Steve Llewellyn was going out. He had just finished as a coach and Albert Butler was there as new A-team coach. Albert showed me to the A-team dressing room and advised me to go and get my gear from the first team room. I was too overwhelmed to go in there so I let everybody leave the first team dressing room before I ventured in.

'Walter Jones was the kitman when I first came to Saints. He was like a Sergeant Major and you learnt very quickly to say "yes Walter, no Walter". If you did that, he would give you your kit and look after you. Then we had little Bert Lawrenson, who was a great old fella. He'd worked at Saints all his life and his wife Gwen was the wash lady who did all our kit. His daughter worked at Saints and they were all part and parcel of it. That's how clubs used to run in those days with everybody intertwined in the club.

'That first day I went to see old Walter and said that I had just signed for Saints, he growled at me to get into the A-team dressing room and he would come in and see me. He was a narky old sod. After about quarter of an hour, he came in to see me. He had with him a pair of boots that were thick with mud. I think John Tembey had worn them about three seasons before me. The kit itself was filthy, it was stood up on its own it was that hard. The shirts in the drying room were more like planks they were that stiff. I made sure the next time I came that I had my own gear with me.

'Of course, we were never allowed to train on the pitch at Knowsley Road. That only got changed when Eric Ashton became coach of the side. We were just never allowed on it, it was training pitch or nothing. That's how the groundsman used to be in those days. We benefited from his strict ways though as the surface was like a bowling green. If you couldn't play rugby on there, you didn't deserve to wear a jersey. The pitch stayed good even in bad conditions; it would just soak away the water. It was always a top notch pitch. We would find little gyms such as the one on Rivington Road to go in and train.

'It took me ages to go through to the first team dressing room. Me and Les Jones played for the first team for about two years but still wouldn't move out of the A-team dressing room. We thought that if we went in there but we got dropped from the first team we would end up back in the A-team dressing room. We thought we might get some stick returning to the A-team dressing room under those circumstances. It was only later when Jim Challinor became coach that he told us he wanted the pair of us in the first team dressing room, that we actually moved.'

Once moved into that first team dressing room, Eric found that the same players he had hero worshipped as a supporter were approachable human beings too: 'The first teamers at the time are the same as first teamers today; they are all just human beings. They were nice people; rugby players are no different from anybody else. I was a bit sheepish and shy around them at first which was only right. They talked to me, tried to help me and never tried to knock me down. They coaxed me along a bit and that's how it went on. That stuck with me later in my career when I was an established first teamer. If a young player came into the first team, I would always try and help them along. I'm sure it's the same today at Saints with the likes of Roby and Wellens helping the youngsters along.'

Now Eric was settled into the dressing room and had sorted his kit requirements, he had to adapt to the level of training itself: 'Eddie Cheetham used to train the Saints players fairly hard on a Tuesday and a Thursday. Prior to him, Joe Coan had been an absolute stickler for fitness. He used to have us doing shuttle runs later to be known as bleep tests. Later, Eddie would have us doing warm ups, exercises, running laps, the lot. No matter what though, he would always have us doing sprinting. There was a cinder sprinting track under the stand at Knowsley Road. That helped keep us sharp and during that time, I can never remember any Saints forward or back being slow. Even big men like Albert Halsall and Cliff Watson could shift a bit.

'Different coaches would try slightly different training methods. I think back then, people expected players to know how to play rugby. They would feel that they could play rugby as that's why they were signed to play for the club. Nowadays, there seems to be a more technical aspect to coaching. Some teams have ended up a little robotic in their style with set plays and set moves.

'Years ago, players like Billy Benyon and Johnny Walsh could read the game and adapt accordingly. Billy Boston was another one with that ability and when you got the ball he would crash tackle you.'

Eric's first coach at the club was Joe Coan: 'He was an absolutely brilliant coach. He didn't know anything about Rugby League but he knew how to get people fit. Take the great St Helens side of 1966. No matter what the score was with ten minutes to go, Saints were always confident they would end up winning due to the levels of fitness. He was a good man manager too.'

The competition at the club was intense and not just in training; first team places were hard to come by. Eric's chance came sooner than he expected as he would play for the first team at Knowsley Road on 18th March 1967 versus Huddersfield. Eric still recalls how he found out: 'I only found out about my first team debut second hand. It had been in the paper. I had trained on the Tuesday and was in work when somebody said to me, "you're playing tomorrow". I said I didn't think that was the case. However, I later reported to the club and was told that I was in and would be playing. It didn't give me much time to get nervous because I was straight in and playing. I hadn't been at the club long before making my first team debut.' Eric's debut match ended in a 11-4 vistory for Saints.

'There were massive crowds supporting the game then

and you would get attendances of 30,000 at Knowsley Road. I think you would be nervous until that first whistle went.'

Saints legend Alex Murphy recalls Eric settling into what was a quality side: 'Eric was with a great club at St Helens and he became a great forward. He had everything you need in a forward. He had pace and ability. He played with the right side. He improved out of all recognition. What he found going to St Helens was that he was a Rolls Royce and he was surrounded by a lot of other Rolls Royces as well. He was one of the best players St Helens had had for a long time.'

Eric recalls his early impressions of one team mate: 'Ray French was at Saints when I first got there and I soon learned to stay out of his way on the field as he would inadvertently belt his own players more than the opposition. He would trundle in and be all legs, arms and knees. They transferred Ray and Dave Markey about 18 months later to Widnes in exchange for someone who they said was finished; Frank Myler. He was an absolutely fantastic player and the icing on the cake for us at that time. He played stand off but could also play centre. We had him '68-69 and '69-70 where he ended up as Great Britain tour captain. He finished up playing after the tour to coach Rochdale Hornets. Frank had it all as a player; strength, balance and speed.

'The late Len Killeen was still at Saints when I made my debut and indeed, he played in my first match. He was a very good player and a bit underrated really. He was a great finisher and if he got a sniff of the try line, he would score. I remember one match where he got the ball near the line and he vaulted over the players then scored. I always remember a tale Billy Benyon told me about Killeen at Wembley. The day before the final, they were walking around the pitch. Len remarked, "If I get a free kick from here (referring to his own half), I could kick it". That's exactly what happened the following day. The ball was still going up as it went over the sticks. I'd say he was perhaps the best kicker of a ball I have ever seen. Coslett was a bit more consistent but if Killeen had stayed, I think Kel's goal kicking opportunities would have been limited.'

Whilst Eric was making the grade for St Helens, younger brother Dave was about to also make his mark in the professional game. He had been playing for Parr Labour Club and had been having a great season for them.

Eric recalls: 'Shortly after signing for Saints, me and Dave played in a works competition at the side of the Leigh pitch. Stood on the sidelines watching was Alex Murphy and I was delighted when he signed Dave for Leigh. It perhaps shouldn't have happened as Dave had met Murphy on his own and was only 18. When he came home to tell us he had signed for Leigh, we asked him how much he had signed for. That was the start of Dave's career though.'

Dave adds: 'I knew some lads who played for Parr Labour and it started for me from there. They played their games on Merton Bank. I was working with our John on erecting the steel. Our boss was a man called Roy Bentlow. He asked me would I go and play in a local cup competition which I did. Leigh were watching and signed me on. I don't think Saints really thought about me. They liked our Eric because he was a big lad. It gave me great confidence that a legend like Alex Murphy signed me for Leigh. I had my best ever days at the Leigh club. They were great lads there, all rough arses. Good people like Rod Tickle. I was the smallest of the forwards but Alex put me straight into the first team.'

Alex Murphy would go on to have lasting links with Dave at more than one club and recalls his early impressions on signing Dave for Leigh: 'I signed Dave as a kid. What people didn't realise about David Chisnall was the tremendous amount of pace he had. He was a funny shaped lad but he actually had a great sidestep. He had a good pair of hands, was very physical and he wouldn't run away from anybody.

He improved from the moment he turned professional. He liked running with the ball. We played him not as a bulldozing prop forward but as a prop forward who could run through the gap. He could go 40 or 50 yards and would take a hell of a lot of catching.

'If I ever had any problems with Dave, all I had to do was say: "Well I'll go and see your mum". That would bring him back down to earth straight away. For me, he was a great signing. He was a great trainer, he loved training. What he liked best of all was when we had finished training, we would always finish off with a game of touch and pass, backs versus forwards. It would be best of three and we would spend ages playing because when it got to 2-1 to the backs, the forwards would want three again. That was Chissy all the way through, he hated losing.'

Dave recalls with emotion the gratitude he feels towards Alex: 'He brought me into the game and showed me a lot. As a matter of fact, he used to pick me up when I lived in Havelock Street. The first game I played for Leigh, he drove his little blue sports car down my street and all the neighbours were out cheering.'

Dave made his debut in a Lancashire Cup tie in Oldham on 19th August. Leigh lost 11-17, he went on to make 22 appearances in his debut campaign, scoring two tries.

The famous Chisnall will to win and determination in competition was now shining clearly through all four boys.

4

Making the Grade

Whilst Eric and Dave had already signed for professional teams, Les was not far behind in agreeing terms with a club: 'I signed for Liverpool City, who played at Knotty Ash, when I was 23. I signed along with Dave Ashton and Johnny Evans. I had always wanted to be a professional player but it took me a long time to achieve my goal. It was a good feeling after trying so hard.

'Liverpool City had a good team at the time with a lot of older players. Jeff Heaton was there who later went to Saints. Ernie Forber was our full back.'

Whilst delighted to sign for Liverpool City, Les had nagging thoughts at the back of his mind that he should be at his hometown club: 'I used to like playing against Saints and there was a feeling of me wanting to stick it up them a bit. I scored a few tries at Knowsley Road.'

Eric remembers those clashes against his older brother well: 'I remember playing Liverpool City at Saints, Les was playing on the wing for them against Frank Wilson. He had a stormer and scored a couple of tries. We only just beat them with us kicking a goal right near the end to win the game. Les had taken us apart though. He could do that as he was such a good player. He was definitely the most talented Rugby League player out of the three of us. There's a lot of things that go towards having a successful career though; luck is a big one as in being in the right place at the right time. I was very lucky; things just seemed to fall into place for me. If I got injured, when I came back things just seemed to slot back together for me, I was fortunate.

'A lot of good players as kids, haven't made it, it's a combination of luck, attitude, desire, will to win, fitness and ability.'

Unfortunately, the Liverpool City club struggled to draw decent attendances to matches and the club started to fade.

Over at St Helens they had drawn 2-2 in the 1967 Lancashire Cup Final against Warrington. St Helens' most famous player had a suggestion for team selection as Eric recalls: 'My first cup final was the Lancashire Cup replay against Warrington and it was a bit unusual. The teams had drawn so had to face in a replay which was a game I was named in. Tommy Voll came over to me and said: "I've told Joe Coan to pick you, don't you be letting me down." You can imagine the pressure I felt hearing that at the age of 20 from one of the game's legends. To play with such a legend as Tom Van Vollenhoven was unbelievable. He just used to go about his business and get the job done, which he expected you to do too. He just loved St Helens and he never thought about going anywhere else.

'I just thought I would buckle down, keep tackling in the game and keep taking the ball up. The scores were tied at 10 all. Bill Sayer got tackled close to Warrington's line; I ended up at acting half back. I went to pass it and everybody sort of moved so I just dived over and put the ball down for my first try for the club. It was a match winning try. Talk about a dream come true. Going up for that first Lancashire Cup was something special; to think that the season before I had been to watch the team at Wembley, cheering them as a speckie, now I was a part of them. It was unbelievable.' For the record, Eric's try sealed a 13-10 win.

Things never stood still at Saints, including the coaching staff as Eric remembers: 'Cliff Evans was the next coach, but the way we got told about his appointment was unusual. We were to play Barrow away and as we filed onto the coach, we noticed there was no Joe Coan. We came off the motorway and pulled over in Swinton. Next thing, Cliff Evans and Eddie Cheetham got on the coach. We'd never spoken to them before but they were now in charge. Cliff Evans was an absolutely fantastic coach. He was twenty years ahead of his time and introduced many moves into the game. I can still see his influence in the game today. All the moves you see teams doing today he started. Things like putting the ball behind a man, double marker, putting the ball downfield and chasing, run rounds and criss crosses. Swinton, then later Saints, did all those things in the 1960s. He introduced them to the game at Swinton and then brought them to us when he became our coach. Once other teams cottoned on to one of his moves, he would create another. He was always thinking on his feet. He was so far in front. The one thing that came in from Australia was the use of the sliding defence. Australia used to hate people putting moves on. If you just play them man against man, they will tackle you all day.

'The fact that Saints had so many quality players at the time made it easier for me coming into the first team, you looked around you and there was class everywhere. In particular for me, the club had an unbelievable set of forwards. You didn't have to worry about anything else but doing your own job.'

When pressed to point out players who stood out, Eric struggles due to the depth and number of great players he played alongside at such an early age. Some memories of players though do come to the fore: 'Tommy Bishop would be the life and soul of the party and was a top player. He was a tough nut too. It says a lot that St Helens were prepared to move Alex Murphy, the best scrum half in the game, to centre to accommodate Tommy. It was about the team then,

Balls, Gloves and Glory

even though I don't think Alex liked the idea. Tommy was a really good player who could play football but could also dish it out. He wasn't very big but the old saying was never more apt: "it's not the size of the man in the fight but the size of the fight in the man". He played as though he was six foot six and no matter who he was facing, he would never take a backwards step.

'Frankie Wilson was a bit of joker. He'd do some funny things on the pitch too. He'd get over the try line and keep threatening to put the ball down whilst still running across. The first time he tried that particular party piece, he stepped over the dead ball line. He got a bit of a bollocking from Cliff Evans as a result.

'Billy Benyon was one of the most underrated players at St Helens of all time. I don't know how he missed out going on tour in 1970. He was playing really well then but in 1974 there wasn't another British centre who could lace his boots, defensively or with the ball in hand. In those days, it was a little bit unfair how the Great Britain side was selected. If your club chairman had a vote with the Rugby League then you would be ok. The two Bates brothers from Dewsbury were selected, one was a good player; the other wasn't international standard in my opinion.

'If any fights started during games, you could bet Frankie Barrow wouldn't be far away. He would come running in from full back with his arms just like a windmill. We played Castleford at Knowsley Road; one of their players, Lockwood, chipped over but as Frankie collected the ball he also collected Lockwood's elbow. Frankie ended up out of action for about eight weeks as a result. His third game back after his injury was Castleford at Wheldon Road, Frankie was named on the bench. He told us that no matter what happened, he needed to get on to that pitch. With about 10 minutes to go, a Saints player went off to be replaced by Frankie. Wherever Frankie went on the pitch, Lockwood went to the opposite side. Lockwood seemed reluctant to take the ball up but eventually he did. Frankie who was about 30 yards away set off and ended up leathering him. He never took any prisoners.

'As a player, I believe that John Mantle was one of the best forwards ever to play for St Helens. He was an athlete, he was a 400 metres runner, he was also a cricketer. He liked a couple of bob too so when the money was on he took some stopping. He wasn't the best passer but in terms of defence and running with the ball, he was second to none. He was a nice fella too with no edge on him. He was a family man who kept himself to himself.

'Cliff Watson was another great forward and I always remember a day we played at Wigan in a cup match. Cliff broke through and the full back for Wigan then was Colin Tyrer. I was following Cliff through and I could see the fear on Tyrer's face as Cliff approached him. He turned a different colour and really I didn't blame him. Cliff was in full flight and he would dip his shoulder and just trundle over the opposition. He used to get himself into some scrapes. He played for Great Britain against France. He wasn't very good at fighting with his fists; the French players were all around him in a scuffle and he dropped one with a head butt. I remember reading Arthur Beetson's book about the First Test in 1970 when Cliff butted Jim Morgan. He spread Morgan's nose all over his face.'

With such a raft of good players, Saints were not only ruling the roost domestically but were also capable of taking loftier scalps. Eric said: 'Back then, not only would Great Britain beat Australia but Saints would beat them too. I've played for Saints when we have beaten the Kangaroos simply because we had such a good side and such good speckies behind us. At the time, we probably had two or three current Great Britain internationals, another two or three who had played for Great Britain and then two or three more who should have played for Great Britain. We had a real strong team. The Aussies were no ham and eggers either. When they came to play Saints, they would put a good team out and we knew it would be a tough game. Artie Beetson played against us as did Ron Cootes. My first meeting with Artie Beetson was at Saints when he played for Hull KR in 1967, the year after the '66 tour. They kicked off, I caught the ball and took it forward. The next minute, bang, Beetson hit me and knocked my tooth out. Cliff Watson and John Mantle had been on the '66 tour and they didn't particularly like Beetson so they sorted him out. We used to play with flair and even gave them a couple of hammerings. We would do the same to the touring New Zealand side.'

The game of Rugby League was a very different animal to the one seen today as Eric explains: 'When I first started at Saints, it was the start of the four tackle rule. So, you only really had three tackles to build momentum before you had to kick, or what we would do most of the time is run it and see how far upfield we could get. Cliff Evans was a shrewd coach and always wanted us to gain ground. The pace of the game was 100 miles per hour. Having said that, there was still some good football played by players who could play football. It was harder to get the ball off your own line with only four tackles. Before you knew where you were you would have to kick or it would be a scrum. In those days, it wasn't where you put the ball in the scrum and let somebody have it; it was a battle. When you got into a scrum, you had to fight for everything. You couldn't just "take a drive in"; you had to play a bit of football. That's where ball handling forwards came in in those days. They could slip a ball out of a tackle.'

Saints were continuing to be successful and Eric was enjoying his career. Off the field, his life was about to change too: 'On a Saturday night about five or six of us would go up to Rainhill Labour Club. On a Sunday, the venue of choice would be Thatto Heath Labour Club. After about three or four weeks, I noticed that some of the nurses from Whiston Hospital would come to the Labour Club after work. We would sit with them and chat them up. One of them was called Elaine. I liked her but she thought I was interested in one of her friends, which wasn't the case. We got round to talking and started courting.

'We had an old van from Mitchells Ice Creams and Mike Mitchell would be chauffeur for us. I signed for Saints and got a new car. I drove to Rainhill Labour Club in it and offered her a lift home. Elaine thought I had pinched the car off someone! She didn't understand how I could have afforded it. I explained that I had signed for Saints and used the proceeds on the car. Now that I had a car, after the Labour Club we would go to the Silver Star Chinese restaurant opposite the Theatre Royal for a meal. After a short while courting, we ended up getting married. We made a snap decision to get married in October. People thought there was something strange and couldn't understand why we wouldn't wait for a summer wedding. We just wanted to do it though.

'We had bought a house and everything was going through. The house was in Blackbrook and was still being built. We were meant to be staying with Elaine's sister in the meantime but they didn't have the room for us. We were a week away from getting married and had nowhere to live. One day at training Tommy Bishop said he could sort it for us as Billy Boycott had a flat going. It was an upstairs flat; Elaine's dad was a painter and decorator and did a quick job on the place for us so we had a little living room and a bedroom.'

Before the wedding though, Eric had rugby duties to attend to: 'My second season, I won the Lancashire Cup again after a rather one sided game against Oldham at

Wigan. It started off a bit tight but we ran a few tries in and won comfortably. After the game, we all went on my stag do around Wigan as I was getting married the next day. I made it to my wedding safe and sound although a little rough. That wasn't the end of it as I was required to play in a midweek game against Rochdale Hornets too. There was no honeymoon or anything. My wife was a Saints fan which helped. My mum also used to go watching me too, until she got barred. We played Leigh and their winger, Joe Walsh, whacked me off the ball. I hit him back and we both got sent off. My mum was halfway over the wall shouting at the referee. She was murder. My wife went with her to an away match at Widnes once. On the coach coming home, somebody had been calling me. My mum responded by whacking him over the head with her brolly.'

Eric's memories of losing his father early in life had impacted upon him and he and Elaine made the decision to have children early in their marriage: 'When we got married, Elaine and I spoke about my dad. I was of the feeling that I wanted to have kids as soon as we could because I never really knew my dad. I wanted to have my time with the kids and be able to look after them.

'I've got two daughters, the eldest one is Gill. When she was born in 1969, I went to the hospital and said: "She doesn't look anything like me, thank God". She just looked perfect and I thought how lucky can you get.

'Saints would play Fridays or Saturdays and whilst Elaine was doing her cleaning, I would take Gill to my mam's in Havelock Street. In no time at all, Gill could tell me the way there, she was only two at the time. Perhaps her brain power led to her becoming a deputy head. Our youngest, Jayne, was born in 1972. She should have been a lad because she was a "bugger up the back", as she grew up and was a bit of a tomboy. She works for me; well I work for her now! People talked about when would we have another child, I just said it could be another girl and I had enough on with two and the wife. It's great because we have grandchildren now and who knows, in years to come we might have great grandchildren.'

The impact of Rugby League on Elaine's home life soon came to the fore as Eric explains: 'I remember soon after getting married, we played Blackpool Borough. I got a whack on the nose which turned the shape of it into something like a letter 'S'. I went into a scrum and Bill Sayer asked me what I was doing. I told him I was packing down and he advised me to go and look at the state of my nose instead. I went home after the match and my wife told me I wasn't playing anymore. Things like that happened in the game though.'

There was no thought in Eric's mind about calling time on his rugby career as he took the next step, being awarded representative honours for Lancashire, a proud moment: 'My first county game for Lancashire was against Cumberland at Knowsley Road and that stands out for me. Cumberland had some real big, tough forwards so you knew you were in a game. Tommy Bishop played for us that game. The county games used to be the stepping stone for international recognition. I had only been playing around a year and a half at that time. I thought everything was going smoothly but it faltered for a while. I never managed to get into the Great Britain side until the 1974 tour.'

The game of Rugby League was tough in terms of playing conditions as Eric remembers: 'It was winter rugby in those days and sometimes you'd look round at the conditions and think "what's going on here?" Actually we did that every time we went on the training pitch at Saints. It used to be a foot deep in mud in the winter. The first team would train on it, the A team would train on it, the B and C teams would train on it. As a result, the pitch went heavier and heavier. Some of the Yorkshire pitches were the same, the likes of Dewsbury and Featherstone for example. Whitehaven stood out as not a very nice place; it was always muddy and a bit drab.

'Back then, we had to play the full 80 minutes, there was no such thing as forwards being spelled. They did bring subs in but it was only two and once you went off you couldn't go back on. If you did get subbed, it was because you were playing rubbish. We trained hard and played hard and nobody wanted to be taken off.

'You could get away with a lot more in the game back then. It was tougher to get sent off, to the point, that if you didn't have a broken nose, you were thought a bit of a fairy. When I started at Saints, I got my nose broken and teeth knocked out as a result of a head high tackle, but people used to get away with it.

'The referees did let a bit more go, but don't forget they didn't have the advantage of television replays. However, elbows and off the ball challenges would often go unpunished. That's one side of the game that I didn't like. I'm not saying I was a saint when I played the game. If anybody did anything to me, I would get my own back. I didn't like people who used the elbow though. There were always a couple of players who would hit with their elbow off the ball; it was brutal. You knew the people who were doing it. Joe Price used to do it for Warrington and Eddie McDonald would do it for Liverpool City. There were lots of head high tackles too; I'm glad they went out of the game because you'd be playing alongside players sometimes who had been hit high who would be asking you where they were and what time it was. There were some evil, nasty people playing the game back then. If it happened today, some of them would have ended up in jail for what they did.

'Tony Barrow played against Eddie McDonald in the A-team once. As Tony was one of the senior players, he was telling all the lads that whatever they did, don't let Eddie

McDonald catch them with his elbow. Ten minutes into the game, Tony got the ball, McDonald hit him with the elbow, stretcher on for Tony.

'McDonald tried to do the same with Tommy Bishop in one match. The next time we played Liverpool City he had the ball and saw Tommy Bishop in front of him with John Mantle alongside. McDonald ended up in touch and must have thought he was safe. Bish and Mantle didn't take any prisoners though and they absolutely battered him.'

There was also a raft of fair yet still tough opposition forwards to face: 'When I first started playing, Frank Foster stands out as a player who was very tough to play against. He was a Cumbrian who played for Barrow, Workington and Hull KR. I've not seen many people get the better of John Warlow but Foster did.

'Another Cumbrian, Spanky McFarlane, also stands out. He wasn't very big but he was mustard. He never took a backward step and every match against him you knew you would be in for a battle. Dennis Hartley, the Castleford prop was another one. He was a really tough player.'

Then there were the scrums: 'Murder used to go on there. If it was today, there would be a few serving time. Second row was a bit of a dodgy position to pack down in as you would put your head down and somebody could easily send a fist through. That would happen regularly. At every scrum, the prop forwards would rattle one another with their heads, trying to intimidate each other. It was just the survival of the fittest. I was lucky when I was coming through that I had the likes of Watson, Warlow and Sayer who were as tough as teak. In every scrum, you had to fight and push for the ball. It was vital to win the scrum as there used to be a lot of moves put on from there.'

Even the officials could be fearsome as Eric recalls: 'Back then, referees like 'Sgt Major' Eric Clay would referee the game as it was and not to the crowd or to the television. If it was a forward pass, it was given, same with offside. Players respected that. There were no grey areas with the referees then, although I'm not suggesting they always got it right; the majority of times they did though. Today's referees don't seem to have cottoned on to the fact that players will cheat as much as they can. If the referee allows you to get away with a pass that goes forward an inch, it will be forward by a foot the next time. It's the same with offside until the referee blows up for it.

'All the players respected referees then because if you didn't, they could make life hard for you. If you rubbed them up the wrong way, you wouldn't get any of the 50/50 decisions. Clay was very strict but I think he was fair. You knew who the bent refs were, you could tell if they gave you a decision that you shouldn't have got. Some day they will do it against you. I never spoke to the referees to be honest and it's sad to see that a little bit of the football influence of speaking back to referees seems to be coming into our game today.'

Whilst Eric could meet fire with fire when it came to the physical approach of the game, he was also a ball playing, skilful forward: 'I did like to play a bit of open football. I was brought up playing tick rugby where you would always be passing the ball; we were very comfortable with passing and catching. That was my philosophy, I used to try and let the ball do the work. Sometimes people may have felt I should have run with the ball more but my belief was that the ball could do more damage. It was all about putting people through the right types of gaps. I may not have scored too many tries throughout my career but I certainly made plenty for others. In a funny way, that's the St Helens philosophy where they play football. It's a philosophy that has continued to the present day. Passing the ball when people think the game has stopped has worked for St Helens.'

The club was run by Harry Cook (still referred to by Eric as Mr Cook to this day) and his right hand man Basil Lowe. Eric's Lancashire selection must have been a talking point in the Knowsley Road boardroom as Eric was soon approached by Lowe: 'I had played for Saints for about a year and a half when Basil Lowe said to me: "It's about time you went in for a back hander." My eyes lit up, Basil Lowe telling me to go in and ask the club for money. He said he would ask them for £500 for me. He came back to me the next week saying they were only going to give me £150. In the meantime, I had already told my wife how we were going to spend £500 on new central heating and a three piece suite. I told Basil Lowe that I wasn't happy and that I wanted a transfer. I didn't really know what I was saying but thought I might as well push him a bit. He came back to me and said they were prepared to give me £350, which I accepted. I have no doubt that they had paid the £500 all along and that Basil was taking his cut.

'Mr Cook was a gentleman. He just did what was best for St Helens. He may have upset people sometimes but I think his heart was always in the right place. He always wanted St Helens to be the best. Whenever I spoke to him, I always addressed him as Mr Cook. He ended up living near me and at Christmas time, would ask if he could have some holly and some berries and I would tell him: "Help yourself Mr Cook." He was just a fantastic fella and nobody ever fell out with him. The decisions he made were not for him but for St Helens Rugby League club. He was involved at the club from the mid '50s to 1974 and the success the club achieved in that time speaks for itself.'

Half back Ken Kelly was starting to break into the St Helens team and recalls his memories of playing alongside Eric as well as his first meeting with the by now feared Dave: 'Eric was great to play alongside at Saints, we had a fantastic team and Eric was a big part of that. Dave keeps telling me that his dad was very small yet Eric was a gargantuan. He could play, he could pass. He wasn't as nasty as Dave but he still had a hard streak in him. He was good to play alongside. If you did anything wrong, he would tell you; I think all the Chisnalls are like that really.

'I was just coming through the ranks at Saints when we played Leigh at Knowsley Road. I don't remember much about the game but I remember being in the bath afterwards and I asked one of my team mates: "What time was the kick off today?" They got a bit suspicious and so after asking me a few questions they got the doctor to look at me. I hadn't realised it but I had been flattened during the game and was suffering from concussion. Years later, I was talking to Dave and he asked did I know who it was who had done it to him then told me it had been him. I said: "Thanks for that Dave". He said: "Well, you were a young kid coming through, I had to baptise you". That was my first encounter with Chissy.

'No matter who Dave was facing, he wanted to win and he wanted to get the better of his opposite number. I don't think that really happens today in the Super League era. He wanted to do his job. He's still got that in him now, he still wants to drink more beer than me.

'When I played against Dave, I just tried to keep away from him. He'd tell me: "Don't come near me" and I would reply: "What would I want to come near you for? You couldn't catch me anyway." He would wind everybody up.'

Eldest brother Les was coming to the end of his time at the Liverpool City club as he remembers: 'Liverpool City moved from Knotty Ash to Alt Park, Huyton. We played Leigh at Alt Park and I must have impressed somebody. Our Dave asked me if I fancied coming playing for them. I wasn't keen initially as I wanted to play for Saints really.'

Indeed, Eric thought that he would soon be joined at Knowsley Road by Les: 'Les was coming to Saints at one point as Basil Lowe asked me to bring him to the club, but he ended up going to Leigh instead.'

Les's move to Hilton Park though would soon reward him with the greatest day of his professional career.

5

Glory Days

Whilst Les awaited his day in the sun, 1970 was to be a key year for both Eric and Dave with career highlights for both.

Eric's came in the 1970 Championship Final as the Saints continued marching into trophy success against Leeds at Odsal, a game Eric fondly remembers: 'The Championship Final was the best game of my career, I always seemed to play well at Odsal. I used to like playing there. The reaction from supporters after the game suggested I had played well, a few of them suggested that they felt I should have got man of the match. It was a see-saw game with the lead changing hands several times and as for the weather, we seemed to have all four seasons in one day. At one point, we put a little move on which saw me put Frank Myler through who fed Bill Sayer to score. In general, my all round game including my defence that day was good.

'We emerged victorious 24-12. We had another good team then with Frankie Myler in the side before he captained the Lions away on tour. He was a terrific player and yet he was praising me that day.'

Always evolving, there was a changing of the guard of sorts at St Helens with a change of coach: 'Jim Challinor was a great fella and not a bad coach to boot. I felt he was much underrated. He was an honest fella who kept himself to himself. If you got picked, you got picked because you deserved to be there and not because he liked you.'

Eric recalls there were also changes in playing personnel: 'The side of the '60s had transformed into this new side with the club selling Ray French. I took his place in the side. I started playing second row with John Mantle, Kel Coslett completing the back row at loose forward. Graham Rees was brought to the club. Saints were always one step ahead in terms of player movements.

'Mr Cook and Basil Lowe were always looking to bring in new faces to the side. They were always looking to buy better players which in turn would keep you on your toes. If you weren't playing well, they wouldn't hesitate to move you on. I always remember poor Alan Whittle who had played nine years for Saints, the club wanted Peter Douglas from Barrow so Alan was sent to Cumbria. Alan didn't really want to go. The same thing happened later in 1978 with Billy Benyon when he was sold to Warrington; he really didn't want to go. If you cut Billy in half, he would have St Helens through him. He was also the best centre ever to play for St Helens. They did it with many players. I remember Eric Prescott being sold to Salford for £13,500, a record at the time.'

With this being the era of players only being substituted when injured and no such thing as 'spelling', forwards had to be prepared to battle their opposite number for a full 80 minutes. The desire to win even overtook brotherly love as Eric and Dave would clash on the field when St Helens played Leigh.

Eric recalls the warnings he would be given before facing either of his brothers: 'Mr Cook would tell me when I was about to face either Dave or Les, "don't you be fighting with your brothers". I would reply "Mr Cook, You're better telling them two!"

'My mum would also tell me and Dave not to fight with each other before games. Worst thing she ever said, because Dave wouldn't listen. He was a tough bugger. No matter who he was facing, he would never take a backward step. We were both competitors though and in those days, if you played and won you got £27, if you lost you got £7. Some of the older players such as Bill Sayer didn't take kindly to you missing tackles for that reason. He'd let you know double quick that that should be your last missed tackle. He'd tell you, "my kids need new shoes, we don't want losing money". He was dead ruthless and a winner. They were all winners at Saints; the dressing room was so positive and confident from the side that won four trophies in 1966.

'Winning pay was a great incentive. After the game, everything would be ok between us. We'd have a drink together and everything would be forgotten about. For brothers to be able to do that I think is really good for you; to want to win for your team and to be so dedicated that you're willing to front up against your own flesh and blood but straight after, it's all forgotten about. Me and Dave both had that desire to win at all costs, fair or foul.'

Dave agrees: 'When I played against Eric, we would go at it hammer and tong. There was no quarter given or asked for. My mum would tell us before facing each other in games that there was to be no fighting. We would be told to behave but things happen on the field. I used to pinpoint danger men and he was a danger man. He was a good player. Brotherhood or not, I had to look after my family as he had to look after his. There were never any problems after the game; well there couldn't be as we used to have to go back to my mum's after the game. If he'd have hurt me, she'd have battered him.'

Dave's competitive streak and aggression on the field belied a very skilful player. Now in his third season at Leigh, he had been virtually an ever present in the side scoring 11 tries. He was becoming a leading prop forward in the game. This was recognised as the boy from Havelock Street was about to be propelled on to the international stage as Dave received a call making him the youngest prop forward ever to represent Great Britain. Dave was going to Australia for the Ashes tour of 1970 even if it meant postponing another momentous event in his life: 'I was supposed to be getting married in 1970 but then got picked to go to Australia. We had to delay the wedding as a result.'

Dave recalls the First Test of the series which was a baptism of fire for a young prop: 'I was the youngest player to play prop for Great Britain at the age of 22 when I went on tour to Australia in 1970. I couldn't believe it when initially told I was going. It came as a shock but you have got to take it with two hands; I was up against their very experienced prop Jim Morgan. The prospect didn't deter me. Jim Morgan was a big 6' 4" bloke whereas I was only little. I had the bottle to stand up to him. I ended up fighting with him at one point. That First Test match was the hardest game I have ever played in. Even though we lost 37-15, I thought I held my own. We only lost one game in the whole tour which is a feat in itself.'

Eric was following the tour from home in the press and was a proud man: 'He was the youngest prop to play for Great Britain when he toured in 1970 and he deserved every bit of it. He knew the art of scrummaging and was a master at winning the ball. I used to read all the little reports in the *Daily Mail* on him whilst he was on that tour. Each week, he was getting rave reviews. He was only 22 at the time and it was a massive ask when he was picked to face Jim Morgan at prop in the First Test. Morgan was big, about 17 stone. Dave had a bit of a tough time and lost his place in the side with Dennis Hartley taking over. Dennis was bigger and a bit longer in the tooth so was more streetwise at that point.'

Dave continued to play a key role in the touring party: 'It was tough. We played some hard midweek games too against the likes of Illawarra. I was a bit disappointed after being thrown in for the First Test that I didn't make the Test side again. I picked up my form when we went to New Zealand and was playing well there.'

As a young man finding his feet on the international stage, Dave was grateful for the support of an experienced player in the party he had watched from the terraces at Knowsley Road: 'Cliff Watson was on the 1970 tour and he looked after me.'

For a young man in St Helens, travelling across to Australia was a genuine worldly experience. Coupled with the fact that he had been part of a Great Britain side that had won the Ashes on foreign soil, memories were formed that would last a lifetime: 'Even though it wasn't like football where they get all the recognition, that was the last Great Britain side to win the Ashes. The tour itself was a superb experience. It was the chance of a lifetime.'

Although Dave didn't find the Australian players to be particularly good mixers socially after games, he had thoroughly enjoyed the experience and contemplated a more permanent stay: 'I did have the opportunity to go and play for a club side in Australia but I wouldn't have gone without my family. I had a few offers from the likes of Penrith and Parramatta.' One can only imagine how the Aussie supporters would have taken Dave to their hearts with his no-nonsense, robust style of play.

1971 was a huge year for all three Chisnall brothers who experienced the contrasting emotions offered by sport at the highest level.

Eric's ultra consistent St Helens side picked up yet more silverware, made even sweeter by the fact that one trophy was earned by beating old rivals Wigan. People who live outside the towns of St Helens and Wigan may think they understand the fervour that Rugby League's greatest derby generates but it is doubtful they truly do: 'We beat Wigan in the 1971 Championship Final 16-12. It was a game that nobody knows how we ended up winning. What we had in those days was that we would never give in. We would always play right to the final whistle. Wigan had Bill Ashurst playing for them and he kicked us from one side of the field to the other. As a result, they were on top for most of the game. John Mantle was sent off and after that, things just seemed to turn around for us. Blackwood scored in the corner with Kel Coslett kicking the conversion from the touchline. There were only seconds remaining and I don't know if it was a drop goal attempt but Walshy tried kicking the ball. It sailed into the air, Billy Benyon went up, caught it then scored to win us the game. Colin Tyrer was stood with his mouth wide open waiting for the ball to come down. The mentality of the team was key. From me first going into those changing rooms I never heard anybody ever mention anything about losing. It was always win, win, win; it was all you could hear.'

The dismissal of Mantle hadn't cost Saints a memorable win and Eric reflects on the occasions he received his marching orders from the referee: 'I think I was only sent off four times in my career and three of those were against Leigh. The first time was playing them at Knowsley Road. I made a break and passed the ball to Billy Benyon. Just as I passed it, the winger Joe Walsh rattled me. I got up and I started fighting with him. We both got sent off.

'Another time, I was tackled and one of their players was pulling my leg as I was trying to play the ball. Billy Thompson sent me off as he said I had been stamping on the player, I hadn't, I had just been trying to free my leg. For that one, I went in front of the disciplinary at Leeds. They told me I had been charged with stamping. I asked them if the other player was injured and had broken ribs. They said he had been uninjured and had remained on the field. I said, "Do you not think if I had stamped on someone's ribcage I would have done him a lot of damage?" I still got a two-match ban.

'I got sent off playing against Dewsbury against a young and very thin Jeff Grayshon. I was sent off for a stiff arm, we were losing at the time. After I got sent off, we ended up winning.'

A key element of any Saints player's career would be the derby matches against Wigan as Eric remembers: 'The Saints-Wigan games were always special. I do remember the occasion we beat them 53-11 at Wigan back on Boxing Day 1969. The game started off badly for us. They kicked off; I was stood on the touchline with John Mantle stood just inside me. The ball bounced between us with each of us thinking the other had it covered. Wigan picked up the ball and scored within a few minutes. We then put them to the sword and it was fantastic to see Wigan supporters streaming away from the ground with 20 minutes remaining. One of our players remarked: 'Give them a wave, they're going a bit earlier today.

'It is true to say that supporters would stop us the week of a Saints-Wigan game to remind us of the importance of winning. It has always been like that and always will be. That's all St Helens and Wigan people think about. It's local rivalry which is good for a sport. It creates interest to have two top teams where you don't know who is going to win.'

Another trophy win took place against more continental opposition than the 'pie eaters': 'I played in France with Saints as well. We played the first European Cup match when we faced St Gaudens in Toulouse. That was an experience in itself. We were away in France having a few drinks and you know how that sometimes can turn out. The next day, we went to the match on a nice, sunny day. We got changed and went out to a little warming up area. The French side were warming up which was the first time I'd ever seen a side warm up before a game. They were running about and passing, we were all sat on the floor in the sun. We beat them home and away.'

Dave, meanwhile, was about to make a lifelong friend in his own inimitable fashion as Ken Kelly remembers: 'We've been good mates for over 40 years now. The thing with Dave what people don't like is he tells it as he thinks. We got selected for Lancashire whilst I was at Saints and Dave was at Leigh around 1971. We got on the bus at Saints' ground and went up to Whitehaven. There was nobody sat next to Dave so I went to sit next to him. We just started talking and really got on. We got beat in Whitehaven which was never an easy place to go. I sat down next to him after the game and he said: "You weren't really as sharp as you normally are Ken." 'I replied: "No, not really Dave, prop forwards let me down." "Fair comment," he said.

It is fair to say that a Chisnall family trait is that they are straight talking and tell people exactly what they think and there is a sense that they respect the same in return.

Les and Dave, teammates at Leigh, were having a fantastic '70-71 season under the leadership of player coach Alex Murphy. It was to culminate in the Challenge Cup Final versus Leeds at Wembley but one brother was to miss out as Eric explains: 'Les and Dave were both at Leigh for the Challenge Cup Final versus Leeds but Dave was suspended. He'd given someone a smack a couple of weeks before the final and ended up with a ban. If he hadn't have been banned, they would have both played in the same final.'

Dave was devastated by the ban, 'I was suspended and missed the big game. I was gutted but Alex Murphy said I would get more chances which was true. I thought the suspension was terrible to be honest. I don't think I deserved to get sent off in the first place and to then get a four-game suspension was very unjust in my opinion. It was diabolical to do that to a young lad. In those days you could get set up; players would wind you up that much that you would lose your temper. It's alright people telling you not to lose your temper but when they are winding you up, it's easier said than done. I was one that would never back down anyway.'

Leigh were huge underdogs for the final against Leeds. Although Leigh were a respected side in the then First Division, Leeds' resources were far stronger as a club and they were able to boast an incredible 14 internationals in their squad. The bookies made them 1-9 favourites. However player coach Murphy scored two drop goals in a stunning 24-7 upset and carried off the Lance Todd Trophy after being carried off himself.

Whilst Dave had to sit out the biggest game of the year and for some players, a once in a lifetime opportunity, Les was named on the bench and recalls the big day: 'Wembley was brilliant. Walking out on to the pitch was like being swallowed up. As you came out of the tunnel, it just kind of engulfed you. Both subs came on that day, myself and Roy Lester. I came on for Alex after he was flattened by Syd Hynes. It was a good weekend. I still have the shirt I played in that day.'

Hynes had become the first player to be sent off in the Cup Final after an incident with Alex Murphy. Leigh went on to win in what Les remembers as a brutal game: 'My lad bought the video of the Leigh v Leeds 1971 Cup Final and we watched it recently. He said: "I don't believe what you got away with." He couldn't get over all the head high tackles that went on. You don't realise yourself until you watch it that it was bad. It was a surprise for my lad.'

Eric's view of his brother's performances that season show how talented a player Les was: 'In my mind, Les was the best player out of the three of us. He was a pacy, skilful centre. It's how much you want to do it sometimes and it's your luck.'

Buller Greenhalgh agrees: 'Les was the more talented rugby player but perhaps lacked the aggression of Dave and Eric.'

As for Murphy himself, he is under no illusions as to the

importance of Les Chisnall to his Leigh side of that time: 'Les Chisnall was a very talented back; as a matter of fact he is probably the most underrated player of the three brothers. He did exceptionally well when I signed him for Leigh. He was a smashing lad with a very good pair of hands. If he lacked anything, it was probably acceleration of the highest level. He had a lot of ability and could tackle. He could also read the game well. He came on for me at Wembley after the Syd Hynes incident. Les was probably one of the unsung heroes at Leigh. Every time he went on he always gave 100 per cent. He very rarely had mediocre days; he always played at the same level.'

However, the ultra influential Murphy was to leave Leigh and not for the first time, this would cause members of the Chisnall family to leave a club. For Les it was to signal the end of his professional career after scoring nine tries in 49 appearances for the Leigh club. He explains: 'Murph left to go to Warrington and Peter Smethurst took over. I had a couple of games under Peter, got fed up and packed in the game for a while. Then I got myself fit and went back playing for Pilks Recs. I got my release from Leigh to allow me to do this. I had that many happy moments at Pilks that it was the natural place to go back to for me.'

It wasn't to be the only time the involvement of Smethurst would signal the end of a Chisnall's playing career.

After making 140 appearances for Leigh, Dave was to join Murphy at the club he would perhaps be most closely associated with as Alex explains: 'I took Dave to Warrington; he achieved an awful lot and was a better forward than anybody gives him credit for. How St Helens missed him as a kid I will never know.

'The Warrington fans give him a great reception to this day and that's because what he got, he gave. He produced it on the pitch when it mattered. He scored tries that some of the threequarters would be very proud to score. He could handle himself and was a very, very classy forward.'

Eric recalls: 'Dave changed clubs a few times throughout his career. His first move was from Leigh to Warrington for a transfer fee of £8000 and I don't think he'd have gone apart from Murphy making the move as coach. He used to think the world of Murphy and it paid dividends for him. He went to Warrington and they did well during his spell there.'

Under Murphy, Warrington were to build a strong side in the 1970s and the promise Alex had made to a distraught young Dave missing out on Wembley that more cup finals were in the future for him was soon to ring true. Dave was to form a formidable front row with hooker Kevin Ashcroft and prop Brian Brady.

Dave made an instant impact at Wilderspool even assisting in a famous Warrington victory over the touring New Zealand side as Kiwi international Mike McClennan remembers: 'I was part of the New Zealand side that played against Warrington. I was involved in a tackle, the ball was a bit loose, I sort of went with a little foot movement towards the ball but from a Warrington point of view it looked like I was kicking at Dave Chisnall. He was shouting at me what he was going to do to me and I was giving him a bit back. Thankfully for me, there were only ten minutes to go in the game. They were tough lads.'

Having survived his initial encounter with Dave, McClennan would go on to have greater involvement with the Chisnall family in later years. As for Dave, he remembers the game for another reason: 'I scored my first try for Warrington in that win against New Zealand.' Dave feared no opponent, quite incredible when you consider the game at that time saw him pack down against some of the biggest, most feared forwards ever. Forwards such as Jim Mills, John Burke, Ian Van Bellen, Mick Harrison and Les Tonks. All these men were considerably bigger than Dave but the difference in size was more than made up for by Dave's huge competitive desire.

Dave highlights some of Warrington's and his fiercest rivalries of the time: 'Warrington had big rivalries with Featherstone and Dewsbury. Those teams liked to try and bully you. Featherstone had a player called Tonks who was 18 stone. The game was different back then, there was no being spelled. It was 80 minutes taking on some of the hardest men ever to play the game. I'm talking about people like John Burke at Wakefield. It didn't matter who it was though, you took a man. Really, you went to hurt them. That was the game because if you didn't hurt them they were going to hurt you. It was the law of the jungle. In my era, it was the five metre rule meaning you had people in your face all the time. You had to be thinking and be on your game all the time. My sidestep helped me get out of trouble on a few occasions.'

Away from sport, eldest brother John was having to derive an income outside the ring which would have a positive knock-on effect on Eric: 'John and I got very close, I used to work on Peasley Cross Lane whilst John was working at Pilks on a contract. He did me the best favour in my life when he turned up outside my work and said: "I've got you a job." It was at Pilks but the only catch was that I had to start that very minute. I started doing contracting for Pilks and that's what I always did after that. I went from getting £8 a week to £32 a week. The only problem was John would never bring any lunch in with him so would always take half of mine. We worked at sites all over the North West such as St Helens, Crewe and Warrington. I used to be his chauffeur, going round his to pick him up. It could be difficult to get him going some mornings as he liked a little drink and would have some good nights out. He was a real hard worker though. As time went on, he did mellow a bit and he would do anything for anybody. That's what ended up causing him most of his troubles. He never went looking for bother but if anything came his way, he would sort it out.'

Eric had seen first hand what a Wembley win had meant to Les and was keen to experience the same for himself. Despite Saints' run of success since he had joined the club, a Challenge Cup Final appearance had eluded him.

The 1971-72 season was to see Saints fight for honours on all fronts. Eric played an incredible 53 matches in the season as Saints pressed forward in all competitions.

Eric recalls the season: 'In addition to the 53 matches, we were working as well. With the additional competitions like the BBC Floodlit or the Lancashire Cup, we would be playing midweek very often. It was different in those days because you got paid when you played. If you got a little knock, you'd be able to shrug it off for a game and put it to the back of your mind. I always worried about being out of the team because if someone took your place and played well, you might not get back in. I alternated between my usual second row position and prop that season. I think it was Basil Lowe's idea that I would be ideal to freshen up the front row and played a few games there. I ended up going back into the second row which is where I wanted to play.'

As a result of Saints' excellent form, a Challenge Cup semi final awaited with local rivals Warrington standing in the way of Eric realising his dream of playing at Wembley. It was to be a tough encounter and it ended in a 10-10 draw. The replay took place 4 days later with Saints edging Warrington 10-6 in front of 32,180 supporters.

Eric recalls the impact the upcoming Cup Final had on the rugby mad town: 'St Helens would go crazy Wembley week, all the shops would be decked out in red and white. Everybody used to make an effort, even all the little, local shops. On Cup Final day itself, the town would pretty much close for business. Everybody was in the same frame of mind. It's not like that these days and I wonder how much of an influence television has had on people's connection with the sport and their club. I think the standard of television coverage is excellent but it has the knock-on effect of Joe Public not going to matches in as large a number as they used to.'

Preparations for the trip could now begin in earnest: 'We would go to Blackpool for a couple of days in the run up to Wembley. We'd go down to Wembley perhaps on Wednesday. We used to stay in very nice hotels. We would train at the playing facilities of one of the dental colleges which was a superb place to go. John Clegg had organised that for us. The weather was good when we went too.'

Wembley week passed in a blur as the day of the Cup Final itself arrived: 'As for the day itself, I count myself very lucky as I've walked down Wembley Way as a spectator and I've been down it on the bus. The bus used to take you right down to the top end with speckies either side of you. They would all be shouting, cheering and banging on the coach. I think our bus driver nearly threw a wobbler. It got the better of him a little bit. Nowadays, I believe they send the team coaches round the back and it's a shame. I felt it was part and parcel of the experience on the day.

'Going down Wembley Way was such an incredible experience. We had to go about four miles an hour through the sea of humanity who were all shouting and screaming. Unforgettable. My heart was pounding, I was feeling nervous. Inside the stadium and then my first walk on to the pitch before the pre match walk round was amazing. Then back into the dressing room before emerging for the match. We got into the famous changing rooms and you'd hear people saying "such and such a team were here last week and they won out of this changing room, this is the lucky changing room." Lucky or not, I don't know. I think they were lucky for us that day.

'After you lined up, in those days, they used to announce you one at a time and you would peel away. The game kicked off and there was one moment in the game that stuck with me when Leeds had put a kick in. It looked to be heading over the dead ball line but time seemed to go into slow motion. We got away with it.

'We didn't play the best of rugby against Leeds. We actually became the first team to score before 3.00pm in a Challenge Cup Final. The game had kicked off a minute or so early. We kicked off to them and on the fourth tackle Hepworth tried to kick the ball down field. Graham Rees charged it down and scored for us. It was a hard game and we counted ourselves lucky as Clawson had missed a few goals for them that normally he might have kicked. That's Wembley and nerves get the better of people. Once you miss one, it starts to play on your mind.

'I made a try for Les Jones in the final. One of the last things Jim Challinor had said to me before going out on to the Wembley turf was: "Don't you pass any long balls." I used to like to throw out a long pass knowing that either Billy or Les would be there. I got the ball, stepped inside a defender then went back out. I saw Les on his own out wide and Atkinson coming in to mark Billy. I just threw it over the top and Les scored in the corner. Jim Challinor never said anything to me about that. We had won the game.'

Jones' try had seen Saints to a 16-13 win: 'Everybody went mental at the final hooter. It was another dream come true. It was brilliant having all my family there to watch me. I remember climbing up the famous steps with supporters patting us all on the back.

'Going up for the cup is another experience. I was still pinching myself that it had actually happened. It had been such a close game with the difference being Clawson missing a few goals for Leeds. I was trying to look for my wife in the crowd but with over 90,000 there it was like trying to spot a needle in a haystack. I did spot some people I knew and they were nice moments; being St Helens-born made it even more special for me. Then we came back down with the trophy and everybody was throwing us scarves. Wembley is just a one-off. We then had a reception and a meal together after the game with speeches at the meal.'

Then came the next stage of the celebrations, the time-honoured open top bus tour of St Helens with the famous cup: 'We came back up to St Helens on a coach, pulling in at a layby near Haydock to transfer into an open top bus to tour the cup around the town. It was crazy. There were people from Haydock all the way into the town centre. The town hall square was absolutely packed. There was red and white everywhere. Winning the cup meant a lot to us but to be able to make so many people happy was incredible.

'When we took the cup round the town, people kept trying to force beer down us and we kept letting them! However, I know there's a perception in Rugby League that in the 60s and 70s the players used to drink loads of beer. We only used to go out one night a week though. I would have a few drinks at a Labour club after a game and that was it for me. Saints never abused the drink.'

Success was to continue in the family as Dave experienced his first trophy with Warrington as the club won the League Leaders Shield in the 1972-73 season.

6

Travelling the World

1974 saw the appointment of a new coach and cousin of the Chisnalls, Rugby League legend Eric Ashton. Eric remembers: 'Eric Ashton was a completely different type of coach. If you performed for Eric, you were ok, he never bothered you. He was a good tactician who knew the game.'

The appointment of Eric would also introduce an intriguing pre match routine in the dressing room: 'Eric Ashton came up with the idea that we should all have a little drink of sherry before each game as it would do us good and get our metabolism going. We had a real character as kitman, Eric Leach. It would be a toss up between him and Tony Karalius as to who would have the most sherry. Tony would make sure any new players into the team would give him their share then Eric would finish the bottle off whilst watching the match. After the game, we would get bottles of 'Champion' the light ale. I'm sure Eric used to finish half of them off too. He would insist that after the games we should leave the changing room spotless. By the time we came up into the restaurant he would already be half cut. He would have a good match day.'

Characters such as Eric Leach abound in Rugby League and tales of certain players become the stuff of bar room legend. One such character was St Helens star and another person from a Rugby League family, Tony Karalius. Eric recounts two Tony tales with relish: 'Tony Karalius was one of the biggest characters I played with and a real one-off. He always got to the ground only about 20 minutes before kick off. His first port of call, upon arrival, was past the office and into the bar for a quick sherry. There would be another couple of sherries waiting for him in the dressing room. He was just a rum bugger. Tony had a bit of a phobia of spiders and cockroaches, he used to hate them. The big bath at Saints used to be filthy. Occasionally, you'd be in there and a cockroach would float past. Invariably these would be picked up and thrown on to a panicking Tony. One day I found a spider and put it in Tony's packet of cigs. He came into the dressing room, went to get a cig, saw the spider and hurled the whole pack across the room. He was as tough a fella you could meet, yet really didn't like creepy crawlies.

'You would get to the end of a season and get sorted any knocks you had. As it happened, at the end of one season, Billy Benyon and Tony Karalius both had to go in for cartilage operations. Tony had a problem with both so thought he'd get them both done at the same time. It wasn't a good idea as it would render him immobile. Billy told Tony that when they offered him painkillers for the operation, he should have them. Tony went in for his op and didn't take Billy's advice. Within three hours, he was screaming for injections. With not being mobile, he couldn't go to the bog. He was constipated for three or four days and he was told if he didn't go to the toilet the next day, they would give him an enema. He asked a nurse to wheel him down to the toilet; he would shimmy his way on to it and would be ok. The plan worked and he called for the nurse to open the door and wheel him back. He told her: "They were worth a fiver apiece." He turned round to see he had missed the bowl and had shit on the floor.'

An era before the full time professionals of Super League, Rugby League players would have to combine playing and training with the rigours of full time employment. It could be difficult to manage as Dave recalls: 'I had numerous jobs to go alongside my rugby. It was sometimes difficult because companies would worry about you having time off work if you got hurt in a game. I worked at Greenall Whitley as a lot of my family have done. All three of my sisters worked there as did John; our Les was on the drains. I was there about two and a half years. It was awkward getting there on a Monday morning after playing on a Sunday. I would be stiff and sore.'

Two of the three rugby playing Chisnalls had played and won at Wembley, but because of suspension Dave had been denied his dream at Leigh. Murphy's Warrington had been playing well in the 1973-74 season at the right time and Dave was a key part of their achievements: 'Alex had taken me to Warrington with him, he knew that I was a worker and that I was a 100 per cent player. He also recognised that I was a team player and that I could handle myself. That was the way the game was in those days. I also had a lot of pace and a decent sidestep.

'Those days there was an art in helping the hooker win the ball in the scrums. I played with some tremendous hookers such as Flash Flanagan. There was the likes of Tony Fisher who could be an angry bastard at times. Kevin Ashcroft was a good hooker. As a number 8, I had to help them win the ball. I was open side prop so even if the opposition was feeding the scrum I'd be trying to win it back for us.'

To Dave's delight, his art and craft in the scrum was to pay off for him big time as Warrington made it to Wembley to face the fearsome Featherstone Rovers pack, complete with 18 stone Les Tonks.

Dave remembers the day: 'I played for Warrington in 1974 in the Challenge Cup Final against Featherstone. They had Les Tonks in their pack. Bobby Wanbom was a brilliant prop for us. The whole occasion was brilliant. The feeling of winning the Cup was second to none. There was a picture taken after the game of me with the Cup and a cigar. It was the first time Warrington had won the Cup for 20 years and it was a big thing for the town.' Alex Murphy had captained Warrington to a tough 24-9 victory.

In addition to the Challenge Cup, the Wire had also collected the Captain Morgan Trophy, the Players No.6 Trophy and Club Merit Trophy.

Whilst Dave had now followed in Eric's footsteps by winning at Wembley, Eric was to follow in Dave's footsteps by being selected to tour Australia in the 1974 Great Britain touring party.

Eric recalls how he earned his place: 'I'd been playing and had injured a shoulder. Jim Challinor told me that it was a real shame as I had been picked to go on the 1974 Great Britain tour to Australia. I told him that it was no use telling me that now. He told me to get fit and that Reg Parker would see if he could get me on the tour. I got fit and was still picked. Jim Challinor told me I had put a bit of weight on and I said I would have to stitch my mouth up. There was no way I was missing the tour. I'd only got fit about six or seven weeks before the end of the season.' The '74 Ashes series would see Great Britain face an Australian side thirsting for revenge after their home series loss four years earlier.

Once selected, Eric travelled over to Australia and the three-month tour began: 'Tours back then were 13 weeks long. We would start off in Darwin, then move on to Cairns, Rockhampton, Maryborough, Orange then into Brisbane before going to Sydney and over to New Zealand. In New Zealand, it would be Auckland, Wellington, Christchurch and finally Greymouth. That was the end of the world, one more step in Greymouth and you'd fall off the planet. They had no picture house, there were no televisions. They had us sleeping in an old doss house somewhere. It was completely different.

'Most of the time though, we had really good accommodation on the tour. You'd room with someone for a couple of weeks then the organisers would swap you around. I thought that was a good idea as it stopped the tour dividing into cliques. I started off with Dave Redfearn who used to play on the wing for Bradford. He was really good company so we got on quite well. I then roomed with Dave Eckersley.

'Reg Parker was the tour manager, he used to play for Barrow. He was a teetotal God fearing man. He never lost his temper and was always quiet and calm. Nothing fazed him and he was a great tour manager.

'We would play country sides on the tour and what the Aussies would do is have us play a side like Orange a few days before the test match. They would put the Orange side in the same hotel as us. They were friendly with us and it seemed a little strange. Once the match kicked off, they turned into a load of nutters. They were just head hunters. By the end of the match, Jim Mills was just walking around punching people who went anywhere near him.

'When you go on tour, you don't think that you'll get picked for the Test side. I missed the first game of the '74 tour in Darwin as I was still coming back from injury. I wasn't in contention for the First Test match which we lost. I played my way into a bit of form in some of the Country games and got picked for the Second Test at the Sydney Cricket Ground. We weren't given much of a chance of winning as it was Australian referees in charge and we didn't get many decisions. One of my standout memories of the Test was when we were tackling. It all kicked off when Jim Mills tackled Gary Stevens who was the Aussies' best tackler and would make between 30 and 40 copybook tackles every game. Jim tackled him and banged him leaving an imprint of his head in the turf. He got a bit of the sponge from the trainer and Beetson walked over and picked him up. We knew it was on, "right lads, this is it." We knew before we packed down in the scrum that it was going off. Big Jim made sure he got the first punches in. John Gray got belted, ended up on the floor and got kicked in the head. All hell then let loose for what seemed like an eternity but was only really seconds. One player had a dislocated finger. The Test matches were always a bit faster and a bit stronger. The defences were a bit tougher to break through. There was no blowing up for high tackles, everything was let go so you just had to stand up for yourself. That's the way it was in those days.'

More brutality ensued when Australian forward O'Reilly headbutted Great Britain's full back Charlton, seemingly in full view of the officials yet no red card was forthcoming. As Eric explains: 'An Australian referee was never going to send an Australian player off. Their referee couldn't lie straight in bed. The referees in New Zealand were the same, completely biased.

'David Waite who went on to become Great Britain coach in 2001 was playing for Australia. They also had 'Changa' Langlands playing for them and he just didn't like the British. He detested us which was ok. It was a game we wanted to win too so we didn't much like them. When Langlands became coach, if he saw any of his side talking to English players after a game, he wouldn't pick them. There was fighting in the crowd at the SCG; there usually was in Sydney. They would have a good battle watching the Test matches. The Aussies just didn't like Poms.'

Eric scored a crucial try in the game as he recalls: 'We used to put on little runaround moves and criss crosses like we did at Saints. We put this move on, a gap opened and I went sailing through at the famous Sydney Cricket Ground. I pinned my ears back and scored right under the sticks. As for my pace for my try, it goes back to when I was a kid. When the bobby chases you, you soon learn to run faster.

We used to practise sprinting for hours on end. We would do it at every training session at Saints. We all seemed to have pace in that side. I always wanted to win those sprint sessions. Same as when we played tick and pass, if I made a break and one of the wingers was chasing me I would do everything I could to prevent them from catching me. You've got to do things instinctively. We ended up winning the game.'

One star of the British side in the Second Test victory was forward Colin Dixon, referred to by the Australian TV commentators as 'the only coloured player in the Great Britain side'. Eric remembers the tough forward: 'The only way Colin Dixon was treated differently wasn't from him being black but because he was a good player. When we played Salford, I always got stuck into him as he was fantastic. You've always got to try and stifle the best players straight away. I knew Colin from 1966 when he played for Halifax in the Championship Final. He was a very aggressive player and would not back down to anybody. He was a tough man and a gentleman off the field. You play against these players and you don't like them because they're good players. It's them or you, win or lose. When you get to know them properly, they're the same as anybody, they are really nice people, just salt of the earth Rugby League players. They were dead honest, genuine people.'

Another key performer for the British side that day was half back Steve Nash as Eric outlines: 'Steve Nash was a tremendous half back. He was around 5ft 6ins and played as if he was 6ft 6ins. There were some fantastic half backs in the game at that time such as Reggie Bowden. The majority of teams seemed to have a really good stand off or scrum half. They had to be tough as the game wasn't easy in the '60s and '70s. Playing against the likes of Bobby Fulton and Tommy Raudonikis you had to be up to the mark.'

The Ashes series was level at one game all.

'It was all on for the last deciding Test match. We had a bit of a makeshift team as Roger Millward was playing on the wing. We played really well and were there or thereabouts considering our injury problems. In the second half though, Don Lancaster, the Australian referee, gave them everything. Whenever we built up any kind of momentum the ref would award them a free kick and we'd be defending again. All three Test matches were close games though.'

Eric remembers one key moment that could have changed the game: 'I charged the ball down in the Third Test, with it being an oval I couldn't get my bearings whether I was going straight or sideways. If it had been an ordinary pitch, I'd have been able to pick up the ball and probably score. I was a bit disorientated though and the chance went.'

So, the history books reveal that the Lions lost 6-12 at Brisbane in the First Test, but in Sydney pulled off a marvellous 16-11 success. Eric who was playing in the second row scored a try on his Test debut. Unfortunately, the Aussies pipped the Lions 18-22 in the Third Test in Sydney, before 55,505 fans.

The New Zealand leg of the tour saw an unusual enforced team selection for the Lions: 'Jim Challinor was Great Britain coach at the time. He ended up playing for Great Britain on that tour and he was about 45. It happened when we were over in New Zealand in one of the Maori strongholds. He scored two tries too! He was in line for a jersey in the next Test the way he was playing. I think it was one of his little ambitions to have another little go. Whilst he had been coach at Saints though, he would always train and was very fit. He was in his mid 40s when making his short comeback at international level. It was his downfall though. He was Oldham coach at the time and when he returned back off the tour he played in a testimonial fixture. He got a bang in his back and they believe that might have been what triggered his cancer.'

Eric's lasting memories of the tour are those of friendships forged and shared experiences over the 13 weeks: 'My main memories from the tour are of the camaraderie we had between us and that I was away with a bunch of really good players. It was good to get to know people I never thought I'd get on with. One example was John Atkinson from Leeds; I used to hate him because he was a good player. I got to know him on the tour and we are still friends to this day. Everyone was really tight knit.'

Overall, Eric made 18 appearances on tour, scoring three tries. Great Britain may have failed in their bid to retain the Ashes but the Lions went on to win the mini-series with New Zealand 2-1, with Eric playing in the latter two Test matches at Christchurch (17-8) and Auckland (20-0). His ability to play at the very top was never in question, although Eric never played in the Great Britain jersey after the tour.

The presence of Eric and other Saints players on the tour had the knock-on effect of wage negotiations when back at St Helens. Eric explains how the process worked: 'If you were playing well you would go in for a backhander when you maybe needed something for your house. If your timing was right you would get one. If your timing was off though, you may end up spending time away from the club not bringing any money home. You didn't want to be out of the team for long because somebody could take your place. I remember when a few of us came back off tour in 1974; there was me, George Nicholls and Dave Eckersley. Eric Ashton was coach at the time and he knew it was coming. He said he wanted it sorting out as soon as possible. He wanted us done and dusted so we could concentrate on playing. I think the three of us got £500 apiece. We'd probably spent more than that when we'd been on tour. To be away for 13 weeks would cost a lot coupled with the loss of wages. We were given some compensation but not a great deal.

'As a club, Saints used to be fairly good with the cup

bonuses in particular. I don't think any of us wanted to be negotiating when it came to Wembley. We were all of the same mind that winning the game was the most important thing rather than haggling over money. If you get sidetracked, you've had it. It was always fairly decent money anyway so if you were single minded and focussed on winning you would be ok. There were occasions though, league matches rather than cup matches, were you would go into the dressing room and the chairman would say: "Right lads, £25 today." "£25? We're not playing for that." Me and Les Jones would be half stripped and would look at each other as if to say should we take our stuff off or should we leave it on? Billy Benyon would be the shop steward in these situations. The chairman would come back in with an offer of £30 and Billy would say: "Right, let's play."

'We did it against Wigan once and the club ended up playing a complete A-team. We used to have team meetings at the car sales at Carr Mill where Cliff Watson used to work. We all got there with only Les Jones missing. We had just about started the meeting when Les turned up with Joe Bentley, the reporter from the *Daily Express* just behind him. He had followed Les who had inadvertently brought him straight to us so he got the scoop. The St Helens people backed us as I think they thought the thing to do was to stand up for your rights.

'The club changed things eventually so that you got set money and so knew what you would be getting. This stopped the players going into dispute with the club the week of a game. Rugby League has always been a game where you are a piece of meat; you try and get as much as you can, they try and get as much out of you as they can whilst giving you as little as possible.'

There is no doubting that Eric earned the raise he was given: 'I remember us playing at Wakefield when Eric Ashton was coach. I tackled the winger in the corner and when I looked at my finger, the bone was up in one direction and down in another. I couldn't pull it back into position because it was sticking out at different angles. Ken Henthorne, the physio, took me into the dressing room. He was pulling the finger one way whilst I was pulling it the other. It took a good while but we eventually sorted it. I hadn't been replaced and Eric Ashton told me to go straight back on. My finger was throbbing.'

1975 would see both Eric and Dave again require their passports for more international duty but hugely important domestic games came first. Eric's Saints were unstoppable in the league campaign as he recalls: 'Saints won the championship in 74/75 season and I scored 12 tries, my highest tally. We won the league by nine points that year. We had such a great side then. I could have scored more tries to be honest but sometimes would be near the line and pass it to Les Jones instead. I always thought a forward's job was tackling and creating tries for other people. Scoring tries was very often being in the right place at the right time. At the start of my Saints career, hooker Bill Sayer used to score tries for fun. I used to think to myself that I was as fit as a butcher's dog, was running around all over the pitch yet Sayer kept scoring all the tries. He was just using his brain, would follow the ball then get hold of it and go over. Saints won the league because we had such a good side then. We had a powerful pack and some great backs. Once you get into the way of winning, it forms a habit. We did have luck on our side too though as we didn't have a lot of injuries that season. A lot of our players played at least 40 games that season. We had really good team spirit too.'

Dave, meanwhile, was to make back to back Wembley appearances as Warrington made it to the final to face derby rivals Widnes. Murphy's Warrington, buoyed by their cup success the previous year, were confident, perhaps too confident as Dave himself admits: 'I captained Warrington in the final against Widnes and it was tremendous leading the side out at Wembley. I think that we were too cocky after winning it the year before. No disrespect to Alex but I don't think our training was up to the standard that he had give us in the past. Maybe it was the players' fault for not giving enough. It was one of those things and we just couldn't believe it. All of us were very disappointed. Nothing seemed to click for us on the day but that's life. Widnes had players like Doug Laughton and Jim Mills at the time. Playing against Jim Mills never bothered me. I took him on just as I took on everybody else. I recall walking away after one scrum and he kicked me up the arse.'

The match was a physical encounter between the two local rivals. Despite John Bevan giving Warrington an early lead Widnes fought back through a Jim Mills try. The kicking of Ray Dutton would see Widnes eventually run out 14-7 winners meaning Widnes skipper Doug Laughton lifted the famous trophy.

Having been on the winning side the year before, Dave now experienced the desolate feeling of sitting on the Wembley turf. It was no place for runners up. A born winner, Dave sums up the feeling succinctly and in true straightforward fashion: 'When you win, the night of the Cup Final is fantastic; if you've lost it's shit.'

Dave had little time to absorb the defeat as 1975 saw the Rugby League World Cup contested between England, Wales, France, Australia and New Zealand in matches across the globe throughout the year. Dave and Eric were both selected for the England squad.

Eric recalls an early match versus France: 'I played for England against France away in Perpignan. They had a half decent side in those days. The big advantage they had was the French referees who were a bit dubious to say the least. They didn't really play to the rules, they played to their own.' England defeated France 20-2.

The theme of 'home' referees having an influence on results would continue when the antipodean series of matches took place. The first match in Australia was between England and Wales, a game that had been built up heavily in the Australian media with comments exchanged between both nations' coaching staff. It is a game vivid in its brutality and resonates to this day with Eric, Dave and then England coach Alex Murphy who recalls: 'We played Wales and it was a battle. Wales had a coach called Les Pearce. They had a tremendous pack of forwards; real physical. They had Fisher who was an animal alongside 'Big' Jim, Bobby Wanbom and John Mantle. We played them in Australia in the World Cup. Within 10 minutes, we had three players in hospital. They just took us to pieces. They hit everything that stood up. It cost us the World Cup. We later beat both Australia and New Zealand. I think everybody thought the Wales game was a formality. I think the game was Wales' World Cup.' The regret in Murphy's voice is clear over 30 years later at the opportunity missed. Wales had claimed a 12-7 victory over the English.

Eric recalls the battlefield scenario: 'For the 1975 World Cup, they didn't have neutral referees. They let us and Wales knock seven kinds of crap out of each other in Lang Park. There was an Aussie referee who let everything go. They kicked off, Keith Fielding caught the ball and I've never seen a bloke go horizontal so quick in all my life. He had got battered when he took the ball in. Bobby Wanbom levelled him. It was like that from start to finish, there was very little rugby in it. It was a battle. To be fair though, Wales had a good team in those days.

'Their forwards: Jim Mills, Tony Fisher, John Mantle, Colin Dixon, were all assassins that day! Poor Mick Morgan, every time he got the ball, they elbowed him. We were having to carry the poor bugger from scrum to scrum. The Aussie referee merrily waved play on. The Aussies were due to play Wales just a few days later and I'm sure it suited them to have us beat the crap out of each other. There was blood everywhere.'

Such carnage would have wilted lesser men but one gets the sense Dave might have even enjoyed the game: 'Against Wales in that World Cup, I was part of a front row with Morgan and Coulman taking on a Welsh pack of Mills, Dixon, Mantle, Fisher and Wanbom. It was brutal but it didn't bother me. I wasn't very big as a prop but I could hold my own. Nobody frightened me.'

A clash with New Zealand brought different challenges as Eric remembers: 'New Zealand were a different kettle of fish, we played them at Carlaw Park. It was like a bog. It was a foot deep in mud which suited them and their type of players.' The match ended in a 17-17 draw.

In the final match of the tournament England lost at Headingley to Australia 25-0. Eric recalls: 'It was a different type of game as the Aussies were pretty decent footballers. They liked their defence and that was what they had built their reputation on. Defence was everything to them whereas we were all about attack. At that time though, the Aussies were just starting to find some kind of decent team. They had the likes of Coote, Beetson, Fulton and Langlands.'

Having spent time away with both brothers Alex Murphy reflects on their differing approaches: 'Eric was the type of player who always wanted to do it, David always wanted to win. Eric was a happy go lucky lad but Dave was more serious. He was proud to play for his country.'

Prior to the home leg of the tournament, the England touring party travelled to Papua New Guinea. It was quite an experience for the Chisnall brothers. Eric remembers well: 'We played against Papua New Guinea after the tournament. What an experience! We landed at Port Moresby and stayed in army barracks right at the side of the jungle. We got into our rooms quickly and locked the doors. We were in camp beds, sleeping on mattresses covered in urine stains. We just had to put our sheets over them and get on with it. Our first meal was in the sergeants' mess. The Sergeant Major told us he wanted us to mix with his sergeants. They brought the food out which was like a bowl of dishwater with some little bits of fish stuck in it. I don't like fish at the best of times. I commented to another player: "Never mind a week, I'm not going to last a day here, I'll starve."

'They took us around the markets. They were selling dead dogs for food, using buckets of dirty water to keep the dogs cool a bit. Later that same day, we ended up going to a reception with the British High Commissioner. It was in a big hall and there were a few English people there. I remember one woman called Winnie who had moved over there from Burnley. Her husband was a brickie and used to do building work. I was telling her how bad the food was. She said that she had loads of sausages, eggs, bacon and chips. She said I could come back and she would cook me something. Come back? We didn't like leaving their place. She used to feed us up and was a really nice woman.

'When it came to the match, there were more people up in the trees outside the ground than there were inside. As we headed out on to the pitch, Les Dyl had a camera with him. He was getting us all to wave to them up in the trees. He kept on pretending to take their photo then shaking his head. They were going bananas at this. Once the game kicked off, we built up a good lead. The manager, Bill Oxley from Barrow, was at the back of the sticks behind the try line. He was shouting to us: "Let them score or they are going to kill us." The crowd were screaming like mad and in the end, their team did score. Ex professional player Tommy Smales was our physio for the trip; he had paid his own way over. He had always wanted to play and talked Murphy into letting him. His first tackle levelled one of their players. Uh oh! It was a bit frightening really. Whilst we were over there, an Australian man had been driving and had accidentally knocked down one of the locals and killed him. He got out of his car to see how the person was. As he did so, other locals appeared and hacked him to death. It was still very primitive when we went.' England had beaten the Kumuls 40-12 in Papua New Guinea's first ever test match

'After the game we went to a reception and there was a tribal king there. He said: "You beat us today because you were too big and strong. We used to be big and strong but back then we used to eat human beings, we wouldn't mind Dave Chisnall in the pot!"'

Dave avoided the cooking pot but it was very nearly a case of out of the pot and into the fire after arranging what turned out to be a near explosive meeting between coach Murphy and older brother Eric: 'I was in Australia and Dave had told me he wanted to set up a meeting between me and Murphy. He said that Warrington wanted to sign me. I ended up in a motor club in Sydney with Alex. He asked me to come to Warrington and I said I didn't want to as I was about to enter my 10th year at Saints and was due a testimonial. He asked me how much I would get for that and I said about six grand. He said: "Six grand? You're no good anyway." I was about to give him a dig but our Dave just stopped me. I'd have been home on the next plane.'

Whilst negotiations with Warrington proved to be a non-starter Eric was a forward at the peak of his powers and other offers came in to try and tempt him away from Knowsley Road.

'George Fairbairn tried to sign me for Wigan. I knew him as we had been on that 1975 tour together. We got on well on that tour and even went on a trip up into the mountains in Lae, Papua New Guinea. It was just a little town and there wasn't much there. We stopped at this bloke's house. There was only one bed so one of us had that and the other had to sleep on the floor. It was a bit primitive but I got the bed. We went to one of the local schools where the kids were playing Rugby League and we did a little bit of coaching. George ended up as player coach in the full back position at Wigan. He was still a decent player and ended up at Hull KR after that. He used to ring me up and ask what I was doing and whether I would go to Wigan. I would always tell him to bugger off and that I wasn't interested. I was happy where I was and didn't want to go to Wigan. In the end, he got the message.

'Doug Laughton was another one who somehow managed to get word to me that he was interested in signing me for Widnes. They were looking to strengthen their side at the time. I went out for a beer with Douggie and Mal Aspey; Douggie tried his best to get me to sign. Douggie was a good coach and a good player; I thought he must think something about me if he was trying to sign me. It helps your ego a little bit. I didn't go but they got hold of Eric Prescott and Les Gorley. Widnes won a couple of Challenge Cups after that point and did well but I never had any intentions of going to sign for anybody else.'

Eric's love for the St Helens club meant that other suitors were wasting their time. Dave though was to change clubs and move away from mentor Murphy at Warrington to join Austin Rhodes' Swinton. It wasn't a happy move as Dave remembers: 'Swinton had a couple of internationals at the time but it just never clicked for me. I was never funny with anybody; I always got on with people wherever I went. It's just that some places don't suit you. It was the worst thing I ever did. I moved clubs quite a bit. The process was quite simple, I would request to be put on the transfer list and would then have to bide my time playing in the A-team until a move was arranged. I didn't really enjoy my time at Swinton though.' Dave transferred back to first club Leigh, scoring a try on his second debut, a 41-13 Lancashire Cup defeat of Whitehaven, one of two that season from 26 games. In total he made 166 games over his two spells with Leigh, scoring 28 tries.

7

Brothers-in-Arms

Life on and off the park was going well for Eric in 1976 with the business he runs to this day: 'I used to work on site, I was a welder by trade. I would travel wherever the job took me. I was lucky as I ended up at places for three or four years sometimes. It wasn't long hours and it wasn't really hard work so I was fortunate. At one job I worked, Frankie Myler's brother was supervisor. I used to weld pipes at the oil refinery. Sometimes I would be working seven days a week. That's just what I had to do as sometimes a contract would come to an end and I could find myself out of work for a couple of weeks. As I was playing rugby, I couldn't claim dole money and had to look after myself. I was very lucky though as I ended up with quite a few decent jobs. In 1976, I started my own business with a couple of folks. I was working for a firm in Widnes that went into liquidation and we just carried on doing their work. The business went on from there for us. I'm still going with the business to this day.'

More success would follow on the field with St Helens first claiming the Premiership in 1976: 'We beat Salford and I beat three defenders to score under the sticks and win us the game. The thing I remember most about that game though is not me scoring but when John Butler made a break. Our full back Geoff Pimblett was defending. Butler had the flyer Fielding outside him. Butler dummied Geoff but Geoff wasn't one for taking dummies and he tackled him. That moment seemed to change the game completely and was a real turning point.'

As a result of Saints' excellent form, a Challenge Cup semi final awaited with Keighley. It was to be a tough encounter: 'Semi finals of the Challenge Cup were the worst place to be. We played Keighley and we should have slaughtered them but we struggled from the kick off to the final whistle. Believe me, when that final whistle did go, we were very relieved. It had been a hard game and maybe we had taken it a little lightly. We were all over the moon with the result though'

More glory was to follow as Saints were headed to Wembley again, but the general consensus amongst pundits was that Widnes' young guns would follow up their Wembley success over Warrington with another win over Saints' ageing stars as Eric remembers: 'Before the 1976 Wembley final against Widnes, the press dubbed us 'Dad's Army' due to the age of our players. Alex Murphy countered this in his own inimitable fashion by saying if we lost, he would dive off the top of Runcorn Bridge. We were all confident as players. We went down to London and I used to room with Jeff Heaton. We were having various discussions about the final and it came back to the same conclusion; we felt that there was no way that Widnes could beat us. They had a young set of forwards who we felt were there to be knocked about. They had a few players who weren't blessed with the toughest of characters. We played on that and tried to soften them up a little bit.'

Not only did the players have to contend with the experience of playing at Wembley against top class opposition but the scorching summer of 1976 was to also play its part.

'It was over 100 degrees on the pitch. The daft thing about it is that the players weren't allowed to have a drink of water during the match. Nowadays, this would be regarded as quite dangerous. We were all dehydrated and exhausted by the end of the match. All we got back then was a cup of tea at half time! After the hooter sounded, I crashed to the floor and couldn't get back up for a bit as I was so tired. Despite the blistering heat, the pace of the game had been relentless. There was none of this 12 interchanges with four substitutes. If a player left the field, he could not return and there were only two subs! If you were playing well, you played the full 80 minutes.'

An Eddie Cunningham try had seen Saints open the scoring wih Ray Dutton's kicking narrowing the gap to a 6-4 St Helens half time lead. A try from Jeff Heaton plus two from sub Peter Glynn saw Saints claim a famous 20-5 victory. The 'old men' had taught the young Widnes side a lesson with Geoff Pimblett taking the Lance Todd Trophy after a fine kicking performance.

Saints' had been victorious again and Eric had claimed his second Wembley win. But with the subsequent celebrations it was definitely not a case of familiarity breeding contempt: 'When we brought the Cup back to St Helens in 1976, it was even better than the '72 turnout. It was absolutely packed. There were even supporters hanging off the statue of Queen Victoria in the town square. Personally, it was special as my mam took my children to the town square and they were right at the front when we arrived. She passed me my daughter Gill. She was only about four at the time and had got all kitted out in red and white.'

Another Chisnall family member who was a child in 1976, has recollections of these successful times, their nephew Sean Casey: 'The Chisnall brothers are my uncles and growing up with them as uncles was filled with all the stuff you can probably imagine. I was born in '71 and in my early years it seemed every year one of my uncles would be playing at Wembley. In the 70's Wembley was the showpiece and pinnacle of Rugby League. We would all gather round the television and watch it together as a family. Dave went in '75 then Eric went in '76, I was a bit young so would just stand there and wave everybody off.'

Saints were then put forward to face the Eastern Suburbs club in Australia in the first ever World Club Championship game. Eric pinpoints the main negative of the tour: 'The problem with us going to Australia was that our season had finished in May and we only went over in July. We had won the Challenge Cup so after Wembley, people wanted to take the Cup around different Labour clubs and enjoy it. We carried on training but it wasn't the same intensity. For us, it was like starting the season again but the Aussies were in the middle of their season. I think if we'd have gone straight after the end of our season to Australia, we'd never have been beaten.'

As it was, Saints were defeated convincingly by their Australian counterparts 25-2: 'I was to face Arthur Beetson and Ron Cootes in a good Roosters side. I had played on the Sydney Cricket Ground before which is an awesome stadium. We go back every year now so the Academy touring side can have their picture taken there. I think they've spoilt it now that the hill has gone though. That was the hill where people used to stand and throw bottles at you! I would play with one eye over my shoulder watching them. We lost to Queensland narrowly. We ended the tour in Auckland. The tour had its plus points. Some places we'd play on tour would have palm trees around the ground and you'd think "it's a nice place to play rugby here"

'When we were on the tour against Easts in Australia, me, Les Jones and Tony Karalius went out for a beer and ended up in a club. It got to about midnight and we were getting ready to leave. As we were walking up the steps chatting away, who should come down the steps but Kenneth More, famous for playing Douglas Bader. He was on his way in with two blokes and a dolly bird. He heard our accents and said: "Poms, come back in and have a drink with us."

'We went back in and had a beer with him and a chat about home. Tony called him "Douglas" and asked him how his legs were. Kenneth asked us if we thought we would win the game and we assured him that we would. He said he would put a bet on us and we thought no more about it. We flew back to Heathrow and as we were getting off the plane, we heard a shout coming from the first class compartment: "Hey you, you bastards, I've lost my 200 dollars, you said you were going to win." It was Kenneth.

'We then played against Auckland at Carlaw Park. It was a quagmire and reminded me of Saints' training pitch it was that bad. Auckland had a fairly strong side at that time, in fact they were more or less the New Zealand Test team. They weren't duffers, put it that way.'

Saints would encounter another famous face on the New Zealand leg of the tour: 'When we went over there, we stopped in a hotel. Lo and behold, the famous snooker player Alex "The Hurricane" Higgins was also there. He joined us for a few drinks and a chat. He did his party trick: he had a little cig box that had a slit in the top of it. He said he would drop a 50p piece into it. He got us to stand up and try and do it; none of us could. He put the coin in his mouth and blew it out, straight through the slit into the box. It was unbelievable so we made him do it again which he did, no problem. He then had us playing this drinking game "fizz buzz". You each start counting up from one until someone says fizz; it then goes back round the circle the other way. If you messed it up, you had to have a drink of your beer. The Hurricane seemed to mess up a lot. In fact, the game never got past him, and after about a quarter of an hour, he was smashed. Suddenly he spewed up on the carpet, wiped his mouth and said: "Let's get going again."'

Back in the UK and the sight of a Chisnall tearing

through the Wigan defence at Knowsley Road had become a familiar sight throughout the years. The twist in 1977's first round Challenge Cup was that it wasn't Eric performing such actions but Les. Fate had drawn Les's amateur side Pilkington Recs against Wigan. The tie was simply too much of an attraction to be held at Recs' City Road ground so was switched to Knowsley Road. Against all the odds, Pilks Recs nearly pulled off an almighty shock, going down to a narrow 11-6 defeat. Les recalls: 'I played in the forwards and they scored late to beat us. I was up against Brian Hogan that day.'

The mighty performance was enough for Les to acknowledge there was enough petrol left in the tank for him to turn professional again and he would join Huyton for a short spell.

Far from the fresh faced, nervous youngster who had first entered the Knowsley Road dressing room, 1977 saw Eric a senior player at the club and as such, was recognised with his testimonial season after 10 years of loyal service. 'In those days, your testimonial season could be quite hard work. You had to get yourself a testimonial committee and I had a good one. Every week you would have to be going to a different Labour club. I was trying to think of different ideas and I was the first player to have a sportsman's dinner as part of my testimonial. Bill Marshall, who used to have the Green Dragon and The Star at Rainford was the chairman of my committee. We thought that a sportsman's dinner would be a good idea. I thought there may be a potential problem in keeping the food warm at Saints whilst it was being brought upstairs to guests. I had a word with John Stevens who did catering at Pilks; he had the idea of bringing little electric ovens from his work and putting them in the corridor at Saints. We had a fantastic night. Speakers included Joe Mercer and David Oxley from the Rugby Football League. David was a newcomer to Rugby League and had been on the 1975 World Cup tour with us. That must have been a baptism of fire for him. You would never think it but he was a really funny type of guy. He looked straight-laced but was very dry. He was a dead easy going, nice fella.

'Halfway through my tour of the Labour clubs, a local cabaret act and Swinton fan, Johnny "Goon" Tweed contacted me and said if he could appear at any of the nights for me, he would.'

A look back at Eric's testimonial brochure gives a fascinating insight into the esteem with which Eric was held both inside and outside the club. *Sunday People* Rugby League writer John Robinson wrote: 'Students of back-row forward play could do no better than note the style and techniques of Eric Chisnall. Eric has all that it takes to make a great forward: height, speed and strength. Yet even if he did not have these attributes, I feel he would still be a success in Rugby League. For he is a natural tactician who is just as much at home making tries as scoring them.

'I have always thought that the greatest crime any forward can commit is to charge into the attack in a way which makes it obvious to tacklers that he will not-or cannot-part with the ball. Nothing discourages backing up more ... while the defender's job is made so much simpler. How much better to do it the Chisnall way and leave defences guessing on what is about to happen.

'A shrewd ball distributor with an ice-cool temperament, Eric approaches every situation with one eye on the opposition and the other on his supporting team- mates.

'His unpredictability is a key to his success and his attacking ideas are often quite spontaneous. He knows too well that if you put a defence in two minds, then you are halfway to beating it.

'Eric uses his height to the best advantage. Even when smothered by three tacklers, you will still see him looking for the chance to slip the ball away. St Helens' success in

The four brothers with mum, Alice. This might have been Eric's wedding as his tie is still on!

Dave at Leigh early in his career
© Wigan Evening Post

John's original boxing licence application

Les on the attack for Leigh

Les, Eric and Dave used to have some battles on the field but were close off it

The 1970 Championship Final, perhaps Eric's best game

Eric always seemed to play well against Leeds

Trophy time for Dave and Murph at Leigh

© Wigan Evening Post

Eric leading the attack. Some support
would have been nice!

In 1971, Les became the first of the
Chisnall's to lift the cup at Wembley.
They remain the only family who
have had three brothers win the
Challenge Cup Final

Eric parading the Challenge Cup around Wembley with Eddie Cunningham
after victory over over Widnes in 1976

Dave and Eric proudly
representing England in
the 1975 World Cup

Saints on a short tour
down under in 1976

A rare moment of relaxation
for Eric down under

What the cup meant to the
people of St Helens

John was keen on boxing from an early age ...

... and would be proud of what Martin
Murray has gone on to achieve
© Mike Boden

John at Bobbies Lane giving out awards, Martin Murray is in the
middle of the front row and probably regrets those pants!

Memorial to John on the wall at Lowe
House Boxing Club

Dave always got a good reception
whenever he went back to Warrington
© Warrington Guardian

Eric and a young Paul Clough on the 2004 Saints Academy tour
© St Helens RFC

Dave was proud to be inducted into the Warrington Hall of Fame
© Warrington Guardian

Eric catching up
with Cliff Watson
in Cronulla on
the 2011 Saints
Academy tour
© St Helens RFC

Eric with James
Tilley, one of Saints'
up and coming
stars, at the SCG
© St Helens RFC

The 2011 Saints Academy tour party
© St Helens RFC

Eric with co-author, Andrew Quirke, relaxing after finishing writing the book
© Elaine Chisnall

recent years is due in no small way to his foresight and intelligent play.'

Chairman Joe Seddon added his thoughts: 'It is a very happy duty for me to pay tribute to Eric Chisnall for his splendid service to the St Helens club. It is especially so because he is a local player, being signed from the Pilkington Recs Amateur Rugby League Club in December 1966. I am still marvelling at the tremendous display recently put up by that same amateur club against the mighty Wigan at Knowsley Road in the first round of the Challenge Cup and I know that one of the many good luck telegrams to arrive in the Pilkington Recs dressing room before that match was from Eric.

'Local ties are strong and rightly so, and both Eric and the Saints are in some ways grateful for the part played by that amateur club in setting Eric off on his professional career. I know that we had received from our scouts and local contacts details of a very promising, big, fast second row forward, and it did not take the St Helens management long to realise that Eric had to belong to the professional ranks at St Helens. The reports of his potential were well founded and in the 1966/67 season he made his first team debut.

'Since that time he has totted up almost 400 first team appearances, which shows tremendous consistency, and over the past 10 years Eric has proved to be a great player and an excellent clubman. He must rate as one of the fastest second row forwards to don a Saints jersey and his football ability and cover tackling give a tremendous boost to his team mates.'

Eric was given a testimonial gift of a different nature as brother Dave finally joined his hometown club. Eric was pleased to welcome him to the club for more reasons than one: 'I was made up when Saints signed our Dave; they had been on about signing him on a couple of occasions.

When he left Leigh to go to Warrington, they were on about signing him. It was always better him playing with us than against us as he was a bloody pain when we were playing against one another.'

The move wasn't destined to be a happy one for Dave: 'I signed for Saints but I didn't really think Eric Ashton was the best coach. I felt there was too much favouritism going on at the club. I was happy to go there but I just felt that the coach was always picking at me. I felt that they signed me but they didn't really want me. Eric Ashton barely spoke to me. It was good playing alongside Eric at Saints though.'

Eric agrees: 'When he did come to the club, he fitted in well but I don't think he got on that well with Ashton. I think Dave felt a bit unwanted at times. Sometimes, if your face doesn't fit, it can be difficult for you.'

Dave was a formidable opponent though as Les found out when he packed down for Huyton against St Helens: 'I propped against Dave once when he was at Saints and when I played for Huyton. It was tough.'

Eric and Dave, now in tandem, would help Saints claim silverware as Dave faced his old Warrington teammates in the 1977 Premiership Final. Dave recalls: 'We won the Premiership against Warrington and that would be the last trophy Saints would win until the club signed Mal Meninga in 1984. It wasn't strange playing against Warrington as I would always give my best for the club I played for.'

Warrington's pack was much vaunted at the time and Eric recalls the turning point in the game: 'It was the moment where Alan Gwilliam got sent off. He had been running the show until he got into a scrap with Harry Pinner. Both players were dismissed and the game completely changed. I see Alan in Greenalls' club these days and tell him if he gives me any cheek I will set Harry Pinner on him!' The 32-30 victory saw the brothers share in the joy of a trophy winning performance.

The brothers, were just 80 minutes away from the 1977 Challenge Cup Final as Dave remembers: 'We got to the Challenge Cup semi final against Leeds and only a bad refereeing decision stopped us from getting to Wembley.'

For the second time in his career, Dave was only 12 months away from going to Wembley but for Eric, the most serious injury of his career was lying in wait.

Ten games into the 1977-78 season and Saints faced Dewsbury. Eric takes up the story: 'I broke an arm during the '77/78 season and missed the rest of the season as a result. We played Dewsbury on the Saturday. They were a half decent team in those days. They had a couple of nasty forwards in their pack, one of whom was murder for stiff arming people. We played them again on the Tuesday and they were attacking near the scoreboard end of the ground. The forward in question had the ball and I had him lined up to clean him out. Another Saints defender tackled him around the ankles though and with that he went down. I hit him on the top of the head and my arm broke. I was out for over 12 months.

'I'd just started my own business then with two other people. My wife was working then too and a combination of those two things kept us afloat whilst I wasn't playing. It was a tough time for me personally. The days are very long when you can't drive and can't do anything. I was going to watch games but I wasn't part of the team. I was a bit down in the dumps.

'I say to young players at Saints now when they have injuries and will be out for months, "I know how you feel. You feel like nobody wants to know you, nobody wants to talk to you, you're not part and parcel of it, it's not that. It's just the way life is. Once you get back into it, you'll be laughing." You think more about it than other people do and people do still want to know you when you're injured. It's not that people don't want to talk to you but maybe they're afraid of asking a question that may sound daft. Players also worry about losing their place in the team. Sometimes, you play through injuries as a result. I know that still happens with the Academy lads. They don't like missing games.'

Dave could sympathise with Eric having previously suffered a serious injury himself: 'I had a bad spell when I dislocated a shoulder. I was away for about six weeks. Then my first game back, it went again. I had to have an operation on it and was out of the game for a while. I found it hard with having four kids and no money coming in.'

With Eric missing from the pack, the other forwards had to raise their game. Dave accepted this challenge as Eric remembers: 'He got us through to the '78 Cup Final really because we were playing at Oldham and we were struggling. Dave made a break from the halfway line, side stepped the full back and scored. That made the difference and we ended up winning the game.'

Whilst not many props had such try scoring skills in their arsenal, Dave had lost none of the more typical attributes of a Rugby League forward of that era: 'I saw part of my role as trying to wind other players up. There were a lot better at it than me though such as Murphy. Kevin Ashcroft was another one. But I had a ball playing side to my game too though'.

Eric's time on the sidelines made him a frustrated spectator but did give him a chance to watch his fellow Saints more closely: 'Geoff Pimblett was a good player who could play in a lot of different positions. He was a full back but could also play stand off and was a classy footballer. He wasn't an out and out defender but he could tackle. He was a half decent goal kicker too.

'Roy Mathias or Slasher as he was known was a different type of winger to the Vollenhovens and Killeens the club had previously seen out wide. He was a physical player who was more likely to run over the top of a player than run around them. He was a tough player who was strong defensively. He was deceptively pacy too and scored some good tries for Saints.' A 12-8 semi final victory over Warrington saw Saints heading for Wembley once again.

Supporters were anticipating that the 1978 Challenge Cup Final would be a third Wembley win for the decade. It wasn't to be. Eric feels part of the reason was down to team selection: 'I went to watch the team take on Leeds at Wembley. Ashton was toying with the idea of giving Neil Holding a shot at sub. He kept on saying we wouldn't be beat in the forwards. Our Dave and Mel James absolutely battered the Leeds props Harrison and Pitchford. However, Leeds brought Roy Dickinson on who gave them a new lease of life. We should have had Tony Karalius and Neil Courtney on the bench but Ash put Alan Ashton there instead of big Courtney. That was Ash's big mistake. He put a hooker and scrum half on the bench at Wembley knowing we had Eddie Cunningham, a centre, playing in the pack and not liking a lot of work. Harry Pinner was a very good ball handler. He wasn't the best of tacklers though. I think that's one of the reasons we ended up getting beat at Wembley. Harry was in the pack alongside Eddie Cunningham; fantastic ball players but not grafters.

'We took a 12-0 lead in the final and were unlucky not to score another. I looked across to the Leeds bench and Syd Hynes had his head in his hands as though his world had come to an end. There looked no way back for them at that point as we were that dominant. That 12-0 lead was due in part to the efforts of Dave. His talent of winning the ball at the scrum even when the opposition had the feed was never more evident when he and Saints hooker Graham Liptrot won a scrum from a Leeds feed just 10 metres out. Moments later, Bill Francis was over for a try adding to Liptrot's earlier try.'

Eric recalls that the second half was a different story:

'The second half though, they came back into it. Their little stocky second row Graham Eccles was the man of the match for me. Their other second rower Phil Cookson started running rampant yet if someone had given him a dig, he would have gone back into his shell. Right at the end, poor Derek Noonan got a bit of a shit pass really and dropped the ball near the Leeds line. A try then would have seen the Cup come back to St Helens. Derek subsequently got the blame for us losing but he didn't miss any tackles. It was the forwards really that let us down.'

Dave echoes his brother's comments: 'I was up against Mick Harrison that day. I never really thought much about my opposite props to be honest. The team were disappointed about some of the player selections for that game. We felt he should have gone for more experience.' Saints fell to a heartbreaking 14-12 defeat after tries from Atkinson, Smith and Cookson in a Leeds side prompted by John Holmes.

One thing about the 1978 Final that does bring a smile to Dave's face is the following recollection: 'I believe Eddie Waring referred to me during his television commentary as looking like a "young Bernard Manning."'

The apparent Manning lookalike had never really settled at Saints feeling the club 'cliquey' and his relationship with coach Eric Ashton wasn't the best. Ashton's selection policies forced Dave to request another move: 'I remember I had played well for Saints in one game and then the next week I wasn't picked. You didn't really ask why in those days. He also had a go at me for something that wasn't my fault, I had had enough and wanted to leave but I was out of the game for about three months. I wasn't picked for a few games and then I just stayed away.'

Dave had scored twelve tries in his 114 St Helens appearances. The next stop on his professional career was in Cumbria: 'I left Saints to go to Barrow, another St Helens lad Steve Tickle was there. I used to travel with him. He was a great lad. The team did well. We stayed in the first division that year. We even got to the John Player Final against Warrington. Its been said that during the game one of the Warrington player's shorts was shredded and I yanked them down but I wouldn't do anything like that, would I? The second year wasn't going so well and they got rid of me.'

Eric returned from his arm injury but his hopes of a trip to Wembley to erase the pain of the Leeds defeat were dashed at the semi-final stage: 'We played Wakefield and lost in the closing moments. I think we were in transition at that time. We didn't have the strongest of teams but we still should have beaten Wakefield. Les Jones scored a really good try for us in the corner and with five minutes remaining, we were set for Wembley. I feel a little bit guilty myself with what happened. We were attacking and I passed the ball to Mick Hope. I felt if he caught the ball he would score under the sticks. That would have meant the game was done and dusted. However, he knocked on and Wakefield brought the ball up to the other end of the field to score and win the game. There was a few poor tackles before they scored. The final hooter went not long after that try.'

The supporters were disappointed at the loss naturally, but there was a growing concern that the club had allowed the team to grow old together. Eric feels that with the almost constant success of the 60s and 70s supporters had come to expect a steady stream of trophies: 'There did get to a point where Saints supporters were complaining that we would get to semi finals and finals but not win them. My feeling was that if you were consistently getting to those big games, you weren't doing so bad. There were a lot more competitive teams back then than there is today. The lower teams were more able to beat the better teams. I ended up with about 13 or 14 medals with the club and most of them are winners' medals so we can't have done too badly. I think possibly the supporters had become a little spoilt after all the success we had enjoyed in the 60s. I think some of them started to take things for granted and believed we had a God-given right to win every game. Most of the time, we should because we had good sides. However, little things happen in games that are beyond your control such as refereeing decisions.

'We were beaten at Wakefield one year in one of the early rounds of the Challenge Cup and Mick Naughton refereed. Dave Eckersley scored and was brought back for a double movement. Wakefield got a few dubious decisions and it turned the game away from us. It was a game we should have easily won.'

Refereeing decisions aside, Eric acknowledges the side needed an injection of new blood: 'Towards the end, me and George Nicholls in the second row were getting a bit older and perhaps a little bit too comfortable. We were still playing and doing our best but the club always needs new players coming through. In 1976 we might have won the Cup but I don't think many young players came through that season. It was the same line up week in week out. Neil Courtney came through but he got left out of the Wembley side in 1978. He ended up leaving the club. We just didn't have any progression. We lost our way a little bit at that particular time.'

Eric also reveals that his return from injury was accompanied by his first pre-match ritual: 'Everybody's different and handle their nerves in different ways. Brian Hogan, for example, would be sick about 10 times before a game. I picked up a strange pre match ritual of my own. I had broken an arm. Somebody then told me it was bad luck to follow someone with red hair on to the pitch. Bear in mind, I had been playing with the flame haired Les Jones for 10 years as well as playing alongside Roy Matthias. I've never, ever been superstitious, but that stuck with me.'

8

Changing Times

St Helens were to enter leaner times in terms of success and the club needed an experienced leader to captain the side through some turbulent waters. Their search was a short one as Eric recalls: 'Geoff Pimblett and George Nicholls had both had spells being captain of Saints and at the time, I thought I had as much experience as them. Kel Coslett was appointed as coach of the club and I was in two minds whether I wanted to stay or move on. I met the chairman Tom Ashcroft and told him I felt that it might be time for me to move on. He asked me what I wanted to stay. I hadn't really thought about that so I came up with a figure I liked and he said yes straight away. Naturally, I was then kicking myself thinking I should have asked for more. I was then asked to become captain of the side.

'I told them I didn't want to become captain as I felt they would cause trouble by taking the captaincy away from George Nicholls. I felt all it would accomplish was create ill feeling, which I think it did. It was never any of my doing and I never for one minute wanted the captaincy. If George hadn't been playing one match and they had have asked me, that would have been something different. I was told that if I wasn't going to accept the captaincy, it would be given to Mel James. I felt I should do it before Mel if that was the choice. I said, ok. They then told me there was another £30 a match in it for me as captain. My ears pricked up. I asked them: "Was last year's captain on £30 more than the rest of us? If he was, we all want £30 each for every match last year." "Oh no, no, we are just going to give it you from now on." I told them that they didn't need to give it to me and that I didn't want it. I got exactly the same as everybody else. I'm certain captains did used to receive that £30 extra per game though. I just thought we should all be on the same money.'

Fortunately for Eric and for the club, the much needed injection of fresh players came with an influx of younger local talent coming into the side: 'Some great kids started breaking into the first team in the early 1980s. There was the likes of Chris Arkwright, who was so good. He could play the game both ways, he could play football or he could play it tough. Whichever way the opposition wanted he would give it to them. Neil Holding was just breaking into the side. He was a good player and a real character. We were playing at Warrington once. Neil went down and as he would, he was lying on the floor kicking his legs about. The next thing, his mum came running down from the stand to see what was up with him. Unfortunately, she slipped and fell. The pair of them were taken to hospital. The game finished, we had a beer then set off for home. We stopped off outside St Helens Hospital. Neil came over the road to us singing and skipping. We asked, "How's your mum Neil?" "Oh, she's broken a wrist." There was nothing wrong with him.'

As elder statesman on the field and in the dressing room, Eric's role at the club was not confined to playing activities but also guiding the fledging talent into the game using all his experience. However, the unthinkable was about to occur. After being at the club since 1966 and playing in three separate decades, one of the few to have played alongside Tom Van Vollenhoven then all the way through to Chris Arkwright, Eric was to leave his beloved St Helens. Eric explains what happened: 'On a couple of occasions, people tried to convert me from second row to prop. Basil Lowe had tried it early in my career and it hadn't worked. Right at the end it happened again. I think it's been documented by other people that I refused to play prop but that isn't true. All I ever wanted to do was to play for St Helens, never anyone else. I did end up leaving the club to go to Leigh, some of which was my doing, but a lot of it wasn't. I never thought about it but somebody told me I was only about eight games away from being the record appearance holder at Saints. I could have easily stayed at Saints and sat the year out and played again when Billy Benyon took over as coach.'

The personified 'bridge' between eras at the club had left St Helens after playing more than 500 times for the club; a feat only matched by three other men in the club's proud history. In all, Eric scored 70 tries in 523 appearances.

Eric joined that man Murphy at Leigh to see out the remaining days of his stellar career, meaning Leigh was the one club where all three rugby playing Chisnalls played. Success followed Eric wherever he went: 'In my first season with Leigh, we won the league after I joined part way through the season. Alex rang me up and said: 'Listen, what's gone on has gone on' after our to do in Australia. I got on great with him. Murphy had Colin Clarke as his assistant and the set up worked well. They had a good guy, bad guy routine going on. We played Hull KR in our last home match, they had a very strong side and the championship was between us and them. I scored the winning try for us. We then had to go midweek to play Whitehaven at Whitehaven which was always a tough place. It was a close game but we won, giving us the league. I never got a winner's medal even though I had played in enough games to warrant one. If I had been at Saints I would have been a bit upset about it. I was just passing my time until I retired. When Alex was at the club, it was ok but it changed when he went to Wigan.

Colin Clarke took the job on but I don't think he got the same respect from a lot of players.'

Even though he was physically at Leigh, his heart and soul was still in St Helens as the following memory confirms: 'Whilst I was at Leigh, Andy Platt turned up one day just before he signed for Saints. He was in the players' bar after a match with his uncle. His uncle spoke to me and said Leigh were keen to sign him but what did I think? I said: "There's only one place he should go and that's Saints". He looked at me a bit strange so I explained that if he wanted Andy to go to the best place, that would be Saints. The week after, we played Wigan and Andy was there again. He was being touted to Wigan this time. I spoke to his uncle again and said again that the best place for him would be Saints. That's where he ended up of course.'

As fate would have it, the first fixture of the following season would see Eric and his Leigh teammates take on St Helens. Saints were now under Billy Benyon's charge. 'I played against Saints for Leigh and it felt strange lining up against them. You've got to get on with things though. If I was playing for Leigh then I would do everything to get them to win.

'After the match, the first thing Billy said was: "Come back and help me; be my assistant." Tom Ashcroft, the chairman who had sold me, said I should come back and play for them again as Leigh hadn't paid for me yet. I gave him somewhat of a sharp response. I think I'm someone who has integrity and if I make a decision, I stick by what I say if I can. Maybe I shouldn't have done, maybe I should have gone back and it would have been great. The only thing going to Leigh did for me was that it made it easier for me to finish my rugby career. If I had stopped at Saints, I'd have carried on playing until I was 45 in the A-team. I wouldn't have been able to pack in. My biggest fear was having to finish playing the game. Being at Leigh made it so much easier and I just gave the game away like that.'

Eric's decision to end his playing career was hastened by the appointment of Peter Smethurst as Leigh coach. Smethurst had proved unpopular with both Les and Dave in the 70s and Eric was to find him no different. 'Colin Clarke got the sack for some unknown reason and Peter Smethurst was brought in. He was a bit of a strange character. Being at St Helens for such a long time, I wasn't used to coaches shouting, ranting and raving. It was a completely different experience. For his second training session in charge, he took us into the gym. Everybody was doing their exercises. He told me to stand on one leg and go down on one leg. I looked at him a little bit funny and said: "I can't do that Peter." He said it was the acid test. I replied that I had been playing rugby for 16 years and that my knees were gone. I then told him something that wasn't very polite. I just packed in after that. I'd just had enough.'

Eric's momentous and successful playing career had come to an end yet his contributions to the game had in no way finished and a return to Knowsley Road was still to come.

Dave rejoined Warrington and the club had a specific role in mind for him as Eric remembers: 'Murph took him back to Warrington to coach the younger lads through a game. He was used to nurturing the kids using his vast experience in the game. He would play mainly A-team but step into the first team when required. He could position his fellow forwards and lead them around the park.'

His vast experience would come into play as Warrington faced a youthful St Helens in the 1982 Lancashire Cup Final, a game Dave recalls with relish: 'I came on at half time and unsettled the likes of Pinner, Holding and Liptrot. Whilst I was at Saints, Neil Holding would complain to me about opposition players giving him a smack, I just used to tell him to give them a belt back. I put them off their game a little bit in the final. It was satisfying putting one over on Saints that day.'

Teammate Ken Kelly had also left St Helens in unhappy circumstances and just like Dave, wanted to prove a point to his old club: 'I remember the 1982 Lancashire Cup Final when we played Saints at Central Park. Dave was on the bench and came on for the second half. The first thing he did was go in as second man in a tackle on Harry Pinner. He give him a little tup on his head with his forehead and got penalised for that. Harry Pinner got up laughing and threw the ball at him. That was Dave though, it was his way of telling Pinner "I'm on the field now, you've got a bit of aggression against you". That was Dave's game, he would threaten players. If you stuck up to him, you stuck up to him but some players would just fade from the game.

'It was absolutely brilliant for us as former Saints players to turn them over in that final. To nil them was even better, not many teams have nilled Saints.' The final finished 16-0 and was sweet for both Dave and Ken.

Dave's aggression and ferocity belied no little skill, as Ken adds: 'Dave was an all round player. He could sidestep off either foot, he could dummy, he could take people on, hold them in then slip a ball out. He could chip over, he could do anything. He could do more than me I think. He had a short chip and could pass either way. He could throw a ball as far as any half back. In fact, he was a prop forward with a half back type of game.'

Dave showed this skill when scoring a celebrated try in 1982 at Wilderspool against Bradford Northern as they were then known: 'I dummied twice in a burst from the halfway line. I scored a few good tries in my time.'

Whilst in the veteran stages of his career, Dave had lost none of his ferocity; the Wigan-Warrington clashes of the early 80s were fearsome between the two sets of forwards as Wigan and New Zealand international Graeme West recalls: 'We played Warrington at Wilderspool once and I remember Dave Chisnall stood in front of me just shouting, "hit me, hit me."'

Such tactics failed to endear him to opposition supporters, a fact that did not worry Dave one bit: 'I used to love it when opposing fans booed me like I was a pantomime villain, it never bothered me. I always thought that when fans boo a player, they know that there is something there.'

Dave solidified his reputation as a Warrington hero making 210 appearances for the side and scoring 29 tries in his two spells at the club.

He would once again move clubs, this time to Rochdale Hornets in 1984. He recalls: 'I was part of their line up when they played as the opposition in Sheffield Eagles' first ever match as a club. Rochdale was alright.' Short spells at Mansfield Marksmen and Keighley followed for Dave. He then went on to coach amateur side the Boilermakers which he fondly remembers: 'Johnny Kerr was there and he went on to play for Warrington. I used to enjoy coaching there. It was good having a craic with the lads.'

Dave's long and successful playing career came to an end. During his career he had played over 500 club games, played twice for Great Britain, four matches for England and numerous times for Lancashire.

Dave decided to rejoin mentor Murphy as his assistant at Leigh.

Eric, meanwhile, had started to assist Saints on a voluntary basis with scouting players whilst a big name from overseas was about to make a massive impact: 'When Billy Benyon took the coaching job, an abundance of young talent started to come through. Of all the players, Arkie was probably the best player we had at that particular time. He was really good and if it wasn't for injuries I think he would have got more Great Britain caps.

'Saints signed Australian Test star Mal Meninga for a short

spell during the 84-85 season and it was a massive thing for the club and town at that time. We were in the doldrums a little bit but we had young players coming through. There were the likes of Platt, Round, Forber, Loughlin and Haggerty emerging. They were just on the verge really. Mal coming just seemed to ignite it all and we went from strength to strength. I know he only stayed one season but we won the Lancashire Cup and the Premiership. He also brought Phil Veivers with him. Mal was the best centre in the world and when you get the best, everybody seems to move up a gear. It gives everybody confidence and when the other players saw Mal knocking two or three defenders off to score a try, they thought "we'll all have a piece of that".

'Sean Day played on the wing with Mal that season. I was helping out with the scouting on the youth side of things at the club at the time. I used to have trials for players at Rec Park. Sean turned up there. He was older than the rest as he was about 21 and most of the kids there were about 17 or 18. He was just a natural goal kicker and at that time, he slotted in perfectly. He could kick goals for fun which was exactly what we needed.

'Phil Veivers staying at the club meant that he took the full back shirt and Paul Loughlin moved out to centre. Billy moulded a team together of good St Helens lads.'

However, Benyon's future at the club seemed to be in some jeopardy as Eric remembers: 'After the Meninga season Billy Benyon took Saints on a tour of New Zealand and there were a few problems. There were some murmurings about me being offered the coach's job. I can say that if it had been offered to me, I would have definitely taken it. I wouldn't have coached any other club.'

The coach's position at Knowsley Road wasn't offered to Eric but it would be a very familiar face taking up the role as a prodigal son returned to his roots as Eric recalls: 'Billy Benyon left the club and Alex Murphy became coach. Dave had got into coaching through coaching the Boilermakers amateur team and later at Pilks Recs. Alex is very loyal to people, he had had Dave as his assistant at Leigh at the time and brought him with him to Saints to run the A-team. Dave helped bring a lot of young players through for Saints at that time.'

Alex explains why he brought Dave with him to Knowsley Road: 'He came down to Saints with me as my assistant coach. I could always speak to Dave and I understood how his mind worked. Once Dave trusts you it's 100 per cent commitment. He knew what I felt like, he knew what I wanted. I knew that I could trust him.'

Paul Loughlin recalls the partnership: 'Dave was Alex's number one partner everywhere he went. Dave looked after the A-team and even turned out for them on occasion.'

It wasn't all plain sailing though on Dave's return to his hometown club: 'I really enjoyed my spell there but I don't think some of the directors appreciated me. I'm a players' man. I would let them do a few things and they weren't happy with it at the club. I coached the A-team at Saints and a lot of good players came through.'

Eric recounts working alongside Murphy and his brother: 'I was running the Colts at the time. I had some fabulous players play for me such as Barrie Ledger, Paul Loughlin and Bernard Dwyer.

'The three of us worked well together, perhaps previously I hadn't had players come back down to me to the Colts from the first team but that started to happen. We would get the likes of Jon Neill coming back to play for us.

'The only two we had problems with at that time were Paul Jones and Mark Bailey. We would have away games in Yorkshire and would pick up Paul Jones and Mark Bailey at the Greyhound on the way. A few times they didn't turn up. They thought they were too big for it. On the other hand, Jon Neill was great. We had a match away at Leeds whilst the first team was playing a John Player Trophy match. Alex came in to speak to me and asked how I was for players. I said I was struggling a little. He said Jon Neill could drop down into the game for me. Jon did it at the drop of a hat with no complaint. He turned up and did the business; a lot of lads were like that. They would play for the first team and us on the same weekend. They weren't easy games either. At A-team level, the younger players could find themselves up against some old heads who would take no prisoners.'

One young Colts player at the time is now a member of Saints' coaching staff. Steve Leonard or Leo as he is better known, remembers being coached by Eric: 'I met Eric in the early 1980s when he was running the Colts side at Saints with Johnny Fishwick and Bob Dagnall. I was in the same side as Paul Loughlin. The year before we had got there, the side had got relegated. We won the second division title. They wouldn't believe I was under 18 so would play me under a different name. I couldn't find my birth certificate so brought my contract in from work. They said that was ok but still asked me to put a different name down. I knew the second year I was at the club that I wasn't going to make it at Saints. The club had Bernard Dwyer and Mark Lee coming through at the same time as me. Chissy never treated me any differently to them though. I had my eldest daughter Sarah when I was 18. He asked me what I was doing for work then offered me a few days working for him.'

Star centre and future Great Britain international Paul Loughlin also fondly remembers this period in his career: 'Eric was one of my heroes growing up watching Saints. When I signed on for the Colts, he was helping out. He helped players like Bernard Dwyer.'

There were some humorous moments dealing with the Colts as Eric remembers: 'The Colts played at Hull and we were always murder for making sure the players returned all their kit to us so we could load it on to the coach. It's not that players take things but sometimes they would put kit in their bag and not realise. We counted all the kit this night and there was a jersey missing. We told all the players in the changing room that we wouldn't be leaving until the jersey was found. We said we would nip out and let them all have a look round. After about half an hour, somebody found it under their bag and we had a full complement of kit. We told the players they could go and get their food in the club. We put all the kit in the boot of the bus and went to join them. After our meal, we got the bus back to Saints. We opened the boot and every bit of kit had been pinched. We'd been there mithering about one jersey and the whole lot had been nicked. The lads were laughing like mad at us.'

The senior side made the Challenge Cup Final in 1987 and were favourites to lift the Cup for the first time in 11 years against underdogs Halifax. A heartbreaking 19-18 defeat followed. Dave surmises: 'We had some top players like Arkie (Chris Arkwright). I think Alex was let down though when coach of Saints as there was too many cliques at the club. We won a couple of trophies with the A-team when I was coach though.'

Dave once again parted ways with Saints and for a time, concentrated on life outside rugby as Eric remembers: 'Dave worked at Cowley Hill works for Pilks. He then got the chance to be head steward at Ruskin Drive and later City Road. He did that for quite a number of years and he used to love it.' Indeed, Dave remembers this as a particularly happy time in his life: 'I had some good times doing that. I made a lot of good friends.'

The rugby bug was in Dave's blood though and he had a short spell coaching perennial strugglers Highfield in 1989. It didn't prove a good move. 'I didn't really get on with Geoff Fletcher there.'

Whilst at the club, Dave called on the on field assistance of an old friend as Ken Kelly recalls: 'I had been retired for two years and was 37 when Dave rang me asking me to help him out. I thought he meant helping him with the coaching but he said: "No, get on that field." I thought he was kidding but he explained that he just wanted me to lead the lads around the field. I played for them against Oldham just before Christmas in 1989. I didn't have a bad game that day and Tony Barrow was coaching Oldham at the time and he asked me to go there and play in their A-team. They had some good young lads they wanted developing like Chris Joynt and Tommy Martyn. Dave wanted to know if Tony had tapped me up. I told him he hadn't but I had to take the offer as Runcorn were getting hammered every week.'

At the other end of the Rugby League ladder, Eric was firmly focussed on identifying and developing young talent for St Helens; some finds proved to be golden: 'There used to be a BARLA Under 18s and an Academy Under 19s and they were always at loggerheads. What was decided was to form District Development Associations (DDA) where amateurs and professionals could play in the same team. This way meant we had all the best lads from Blackbrook, Thatto Heath and Pilks alongside the players we had already signed for Saints. We won the competition the first two years. We also signed quite a few lads from there too. We signed the likes of Neil Measures. Other teams made signings from our side too such as Huyton.

'I coached Gary Connolly for the DDA when he was 17. Saints had signed Gary from Blackbrook. He went almost immediately into the first team and within no time was playing at Wembley in the 1989 Challenge Cup Final. After that, he came and played in the DDA along with Alan Hunte who we'd just signed from Wakefield. Hunte had played in the Wakefield first team but we went up there to play with the DDA and found out he hadn't actually been signed by their club. He was still on amateur forms. We came back to Bill Lyons at Saints and said that we felt

Hunte was interested in coming to Saints. With that, Saints approached him. In the meantime, Wigan had found out about his contractual status and they approached him too. He decided to come to Saints and he was a real good signing for us. He and Connolly played together in the DDA, the final was at Hull. We won that year and went back to win the final the second year at Featherstone. Paul Newlove was in the Featherstone DDA side at that time. You get certain lads who get up to the first team and are glad to come back down because it's too much for them but Gary just loved playing. He was such a good player. Hunte was too, they were good, genuine, professional players. They had no edge on them and had great attitudes.'

Connolly remembers the infancy of his career: 'Eric coached me when I was in the DDA. We had a great side and won it two years running. There were loads of lads from Blackbrook involved and we all looked forward to training with Chissy on a Monday night. We would be put together with lads from Saints A-team and so on. There was a great atmosphere and Chissy emphasised that by having us play tick and pass games that we really enjoyed. He just made it fun. As players, me and Alan Hunte would be playing for the first team on a Sunday then we would go training for Chissy on a Monday night. We didn't have to do it as Saints' coach at the time, Alex Murphy, said it was up to us if we wanted to play for the DDA. I think the club would have preferred it if we didn't play but understood we were kids and keen to do it. Chissy made it so enjoyable that we used to love it.

'We didn't do much training back then as we all had full time jobs. I'd play on a Sunday then be up at seven the next morning travelling to Oldham as a bricklayer. I'd have a full day on site, DDA training that night then first team training on a Tuesday night, Thursday night and Saturday morning before playing on a Sunday. It was only after three years of playing and getting picked on the Great Britain tour of 1992 that I finished my job and concentrated on my rugby. It was great getting home from work on a Monday night and playing tick and pass with all the lads I had played alongside at Blackbrook.

'Chissy had a craic with the lads; he was just like one of the lads basically. He's been spotting talent all his career. He knows how to nurture it and push it in the right direction without bombarding them with too much information. I think today's game is a bit too professional, it's all regimented, "do this, do that". For me, you've got to enjoy it. If you don't enjoy it you won't get the best out of the players. I've always said that you've got to make training enjoyable. Chissy was very good at that.'

The affection both men have for each other is clear, they even have their own in-joke regarding a Saints tracksuit as Eric explains: 'We said we would get Gary a Saints tracksuit when he was with us but he never got it. He still asks me for it to this day.'

Gary confirms: 'Eric still owes me a tracksuit. It's a running joke we have that has gone on for 20 years now. Even when I was in the Wigan first team, he would bump into me and claim he had the tracksuit for me. He had promised me a DDA tracksuit to come and play for them. I would tell him years later that I wanted it.'

Connolly is still fulsome in his praise for the support he received at the start of his career: 'When I went to Saints, it was an eye opener for me. I was a 17-year-old kid and didn't expect to be playing in the first team. I had been struggling to get in the Blackbrook under 19s side at the time. When you reach 17 you get thrown into the under 19s and they had a great side at Blackbrook. A few weeks later, I was in the first team at Saints. Murphy signed me as a kid. Phil Veivers tells the tale that Murphy saw me play for Lancashire in an amateur game kicking the ball and said "I'm going to sign that kid". As Alex had signed me, he just pushed me all the way. With Dave Chisnall as assistant, that just helped towards me getting my chance at 17.

'I only played a handful of games in the A-team. I remember one game where we played Widnes at Wigan; it was a semi final for the first team. That was on a Saturday and I then played for the A-team the next day because they had a big game too. I was just happy to play for them, they had given me my chance and without them I wouldn't have been in the position I was. I was just grateful for them seeing some potential in me and be willing to push me. Anything I could do to repay them for that, I would gladly help out.'

As matters turned out, Murphy would not stay long term at the club despite Saints making another Challenge Cup Final against Wigan in 1989. Eric says: 'Saints signed Paul Vautin and Michael O'Connor for the '88-89 season. Vautin was a good player as was O'Connor but I just think O'Connor came for the ride. There is the possibility that the English game was totally different and just didn't suit him but he didn't look part and parcel of it. Vautin was slow to start but ended up coming really good. They went back to Australia before the Challenge Cup Final and were brought back for Wembley. I don't think I'd have brought them back, I think I would have stuck with the lads that got us to the final. I don't think the decision did much for the team spirit. It was a gamble and to be fair, they were two world class players. It backfired on us. We lost 27-0.

'Murphy was a little bit unlucky in his coaching spell at Saints. He's his own man. I think you've got to be like that and if the powers that be don't like it then you've got to move on. He knew what he wanted and nine times out of ten it worked for him. There was just the odd time it backfired a little bit. It was a bit of a transition period again.'

This transition period saw new faces brought to the playing staff including local lad Sean Casey who is grateful for Eric's support: 'Being related to the Chisnalls, there was an expectation when I started playing Rugby League that I would follow in their footsteps. It never really quite worked out for me in that respect. There was a bit of a pressure there but I always felt more pride than pressure. I still do to this day. When I got to 18 or so, Eric helped me out with my first contract at Saints. When I went to New Zealand on the BARLA tour with the likes of Barrie MacDermott and Terry O'Connor, Eric did so much fundraising for me. If it hadn't have been for Eric, I probably wouldn't have gone on that tour.

'Signing for Saints and going on that tour were massive, massive moments in my life that I'll never forget. No way would they have happened without Eric.'

Murphy left the coaching position and was replaced by Kiwi Mike McClennan. The appointment of McClennan would bring the involvement of another Chisnall to St Helens with eldest brother John and the genesis of what would become a breeding ground of boxing champions, Bobbies Lane gym. Eric explains: 'John always wanted to get into boxing coaching and he got a little boxing club at St Helens Judo on Knowsley Road. He only had access to it at certain times though as Mike McClennan used to take Saints in there too. I was friendly with Steve Kearns who was Head Steward at UGB on Bobbies Lane. I was there with him one day and noticed upstairs there was a massive area they had used for dances years back. I asked him if our John could have it for the boxing; he let him have it for buttons. I ended up helping him kit it all out. He would be forever in my factory: "Can you bend this? Can you weld that?" He paid us back because if we were doing any dinners he would put on a boxing show and we would split the proceeds between us. Half for the boxing and half for the rugby. We did one as part of Chris Arkwright's testimonial.'

McClennan recalls: 'When the grounds were iced up and

closed and there was no alternative venues, it was discussed that we use astro turf but my feelings were that they could cause calf and Achilles problems. I got to hear that Johnny Chisnall had the boxing gym just along the road at Bobbies Lane. We capitalised on that and what was good about it were the benefits the players got from the training and the enjoyment. It was a break from the normal curriculum. John was really good. I can always remember guys like Gary Connolly couldn't skip at first, but in the end he was superb.

'It was circuit type training from skipping to hitting the punch bag to working on the speed balls. There was a whole variety of activities as well as getting in the ring with some of the boxers there. They would hold the pads and get our players to throw some combinations. The sweat would be pouring off the players. It was beneficial and enjoyable, that was all Johnny Chisnall though. He took complete charge of those training sessions that we had there. The players enjoyed it and adhered to the principles in place.

'It was something I had done with the Mount Albert club in Auckland prior to coming to England and with the Northcote club too as they had a top boxing trainer there. I believe in the principles and the discipline that is instilled in boxing. The change in environment was good too. Johnny was such a nice man and I'd always look forward to seeing him.'

The players themselves found the training very rigorous as Paul Loughlin remembers: 'It was the hardest training I have ever done in my life. It was a lot of stamina work. They made us go back to back with each other then turn around and avoid punches. It was a reaction drill. I had brought along my mate Deano who used to come to training with us. Unfortunately, Deano didn't look where he should have and Jon Neill punched him in the face, splitting his nose and knocking him out. That was the last time Deano came with us.

'John wanted us to try a bit of sparring with some of the old heads in the gym; some of our young lads were keen such as Sean Casey who had done a bit of boxing. One of the boxers was fantastic and even though we all had guards, his performance in the ring was a good queue shrinker.

'There was nothing on those young boxers but they could probably punch a hole through the wall. They were only nine stone wet through yet 16 stone rugby lads were shrinking out of the queue to spar with them, especially centres and wingers! Me and Quirky (Les Quirk) got the ropes out and thought we'd do a bit of skipping work instead.

'It was a real eye opener; at first we thought it might have been an easier alternative to running up Sherdley Park hill. Once we'd been we were all begging them to take us back to Sherdley Park.'

Gary Connolly agrees: 'When John did the boxing training, I remember the skipping and so on being really hard work. They used to try and get me in the ring to do a bit of sparring but I told them there was no chance I was getting in the ring with somebody who could box.'

Connolly's sessions with John weren't to last as he was sold by St Helens in an almost unthinkable deal to arch rivals Wigan. The move earned Connolly more than 20 years of abuse from St Helens people yet Eric explains it wasn't as straightforward as it seemed: 'Gary was St Helens through and through and when he left Saints, I knew that he didn't want to go. It killed me when Saints speckies used to call him "Judas". It made me think that did that not make every player we had signed from other clubs Judas as well. Gary's heart and soul was in St Helens. He was such a great lad, he would do anything for you. He just used to love playing and he used to love Saints. That's what used to upset me when I heard the crowd calling him Judas after his move to Wigan. All he wanted was a little bit of extra money, not even the same as the others were getting.

'It's always been the case though that if you come from the town there's the expectation that you play for the badge on your shirt and to get your name in the *St Helens Star* whereas players from Wales and Australia got the money.

'It was a little different when Andy Platt left Saints for Wigan as I think that had something to do with Saints losing a court case with Wigan over the signature of Adrian Shelford.'

The training of the rest of the Saints players at John's gym was just the beginning though as he was about to launch a generation of talented fighters.

9

Bobbies Lane Boxing

The houses that backed on to Bobbies Lane playing field had the perfect view every weekend of a range of local amateur Rugby League sides playing matches there. A short walk up the white gravel track would take you to the clubhouse itself and in there, at the heart of that vital sporting community, was John Chisnall's boxing gym.

Former boxer turned trainer Tony Clarey remembers: 'As a former boxer, I've always been involved with boxing. I moved to St Helens and as I'd finished my own career, I did my coaching courses. I was out of the game for a couple of years but as it was in my blood, I wanted to get back into the sport. I heard about the St Helens Amateur Boxing Club at Bobbies Lane. Me and John knew each other but I went down to introduce myself. He invited me down, I got to know the lads and it went on from there.

'I've always said that Bobbies Lane was probably the best boxing gym in the country for talent. We had English international fighters coming through. It was superb.'

John's best friend, Buller Greenhalgh collected fighters' subs at the gym and agrees with Tony: 'Bobbies Lane was a fine gym. A hell of a lot of people used to train there. John looked after the kids. He used to give them a party every Christmas. He would take them to Blackpool and Wales to boxing shows; I remember one year he took us to Ireland. We went to Donegal. The Irish kids had come over to us first.'

Eric recalls the wealth of talent that came through the gym's doors: 'John's real impact in boxing is the number of kids he has helped to develop into top quality fighters. Ste Birch, who was Commonwealth silver medallist, Martin Murray, Craig Lyon, Gary Davies and others. His training helped keep kids off the street; he'd have scores of them at the UGB club. It gave them something to do and some discipline. It also developed their self confidence. Pre-season, I used to get him to come and train our Academy players too. He'd give them tough fitness sessions every Saturday. He was a very hard trainer and he had his own little ideas. He would have four blokes in the ring at the same time sparring with one another. He'd shout "change" and you'd spar with the fighter next to you. You had to be quick or one of the four would punch you. It was about making them more alert. We'd use his gym when the weather wasn't good.

'He didn't suffer fools gladly; he knew what some of the young lads could get up to because he had been there and done that. He knew what it was all about. His own sons, Wayne and Darren, were boxers too. Wayne was also a good Rugby League player and played at Wembley with the town team with Mark Lee and Austin Donegan. He played for me in the under 16s side too.

'John knew with some of the young lads that if they came away from boxing, they would fall by the wayside in life too. It gave them discipline and an outlet for aggression. His heart and soul was in boxing and his boxers. He used to have a minivan to ferry the lads round and about to take them to training and take them home afterwards.'

British bantamweight boxer Gary Davies recalls his early days with John: 'I first met John at the Bobbies Lane gym, known as St Helens Glass ABC. It later changed its name to St Helens Town Boxing Club. It was down the white "rocky road" of Bobbies Lane. The venue was massive for people playing rugby at the time. UGB used to let out the function room and club to people. There was a bit of a bar for UGB workers. You'd get a lot of rugby league fixtures on the fields there. The rugby teams would also use the club for training. The showers were downstairs and you would get all the rugby lads coming in. The boxing club was above there. It was a massive ring, probably the biggest in the North West. John put an international ring in the gym for us to use. The first time I went there, John Lyon was one of the trainers there alongside John Chisnall. Martin Murray's granddad was the first person you'd see as you came up the stairs because he was the person you had to pay your subs to. It was only £1.50 a week. You can't moan at that for training five nights a week. My mum was always made up to get rid of me out of the house.

'My mate, Shane Booth, who lived near me on the same Pinfold estate where the Griffin pub overlooks the Eccleston Mere, was already training at Bobbies Lane and he asked me to come down one night and join the boxing. I wasn't into drinking or hanging around on the streets and all the things that most other lads of my age did. I was around 13 at the time. Luckily enough, I took to the boxing. I walked in for the first time and I remember the smell of old leather hitting me; the smell of the sweaty leather gloves. Up there in the gym that first night were Martin Murray, Ste Birch and Craig Lyon. The three of them turned to look at me. Obviously, when somebody new walks in, everybody looks at them. I saw the look in their eyes.

'John Chisnall used to take the sessions with Johnny Maloney. There was a weights section near the back of the gym. The long, middle section of the room had about 10 punching bags set up. This was all on a solid, block wooden floor. There was always a circuit set out for us. We would have to go down the benches on one leg, then we'd twist and turn to go through the hoops. We'd then run around the bags, sprint up to the top, jump over six hurdles then run round again. Then it would be punching four rounds on the bags and then four rounds on the pads. Chissy or one of the Bacon lads (Kev and Mike) would take the pads. Chissy was the main man and he was the one who kept the club going. He worked tirelessly around the clock to get sponsors for the gym. You always had to pay your subs; if you didn't pay you were out of the gym.'

English bantamweight champion Craig Lyon recalls: 'I went to Bobbies Lane gym with my dad (Olympic champion John Lyon) to go boxing and that's the first time I met John. He was a character and a top fella. He was always really into my boxing and made me feel good about it. He was strict; he had a good side and a bad side. He could be one of the nicest fellas you could ever meet but then he could be one of the most scariest you could ever meet. I didn't really get into trouble with him but a few of the other lads did. He helped keep some young lads out of trouble by getting them down to the gym. It didn't end there though. If he saw them on the streets he would go over to them and keep them on the straight and narrow. He could scare the biggest fella could Johnny Chis. I always got on with him.'

John's nephew, Sean Casey, saw all his uncles as influential figures but John had perhaps the biggest impact on him: 'From a very early age, before I started playing rugby, I was at the boxing club.

'The thing with John was he wouldn't just take me down to the boxing club but loads of my mates as well. He was almost a Pied Piper type person. He was always trying to recruit lads down to the boxing club. He had success with it as well when you look at who came through that club.

'The family do's were always interesting as John would use them as an opportunity to try and recruit more lads into boxing. He was always the star of the show at the family do's. My two sisters have got kids of their own, our Julie has got three lads and he was always trying to get Dave and Steve Cunliffe into the gym.

'He was always after Les' son; Ian Chisnall and get him into boxing. Then he'd be after Dave's lads; Phil and Lee.

'John would be constantly saying that the boxing club was where we needed to be. He'd be in everybody's ear all the time. It would get to the point where my mum would say "bloody hell John, leave him alone". He would pick lads up and take them to the gym, that's how keen he was. He was such a big hearted fella. He would never ask for a penny.

'For us as well, John's son Wayne had so much potential as a boxer. John put so much time and effort into Wayne. He had bags and bags of talent and really could have made it. He had all the attributes, he was a lovely boxer. John recognized that but trying to keep Wayne focused was sometimes tricky.'

Tony Clarey recalls how John recruited one of his most famous young stars, Martin Murray: 'The way he found Martin was that he pulled up alongside him in a van, said: "get in the van but before you do tell your mum you are going the boxing gym".'

Martin, himself, clearly still holds John in the highest regard yet it was Eric who had coached him first: 'I played under 13s Rugby League with Ste Kilgannon under Eric. Eric reckons I used to mither him to death, I can't remember that. It was funny playing rugby because I was only tiny. I was only about seven stone when I was 16 so you can imagine how light I was at 13. I was put on the wing as all the other kids were massive. Eric was my rugby coach and then John was my boxing coach. Rugby wasn't for me but I had a good laugh. It was a good experience. I was clever enough to know that I would never make it in rugby. I'd train twice a week at Knowsley Road and I'd be doing my boxing training at Bobbies Lane. The rugby meant I was missing a couple of boxing sessions. It never came to the point where I knew I would have to pick one as I knew I couldn't have made it at rugby. It sounds daft because I was going boxing where I would be getting punched but rugby is a tough game. You know where the knocks are coming from in boxing. I admire rugby players; some of them are made of steel with the knocks they take. Rugby lads get hit from all angles. I enjoyed it whilst I was there.

'As for how I got into boxing, it was all down to John. He used to come down to my estate. He was just so passionate about getting kids into boxing and making them do something with their lives. He'd pick us up in his van, take us to training then drop us back home. It was brilliant.

'He created some good lads; he was born to do that. Funnily enough, Joe Griff who used to help John out doing bits and bobs of training gave me a DVD of the first time I was in the gym when I was seven. John was on it and it was mad looking back watching it. I picked the sport up properly when I was 10 because my best mate, Ste Birch, was doing it. He was flying along so I picked it up and I never looked back.

'John was John. He did everything his way. He demanded respect and the respect was there. He used to walk in that gym even when he was in his sixties and he would have big, fully grown men up the wall. They would be tip toeing about him. John would just say it how it was, he was always straight to the point and the gym was his place. I went all over the world with him. He had the same amount of respect from everyone who came across him; he was just that type of bloke.'

John certainly had his strict side and as with all young men, his boxers would test his patience and forever be pushing the limits. Buller remembers: 'Chissy had a short fuse. He had a massive impact on Martin even though they used to fight like cat and dog; they were always arguing.

Martin thought the world of him though.

'Chissy wouldn't have any messing about in the gym. He was always serious. Some of the kids would have ended up in trouble if it hadn't have been for them. Boxing was his life.'

Gary Davies agrees: 'He was good at what he did. It's not like today where if you don't turn up at the gym the trainer isn't arsed because it's your own problem. John would be knocking on your door if you didn't turn up. I remember Birchy used to struggle to get out of bed of a morning and John would be banging on the door to get him out of his flat. One day Birchy would be getting grief off John, the next day it would be Martin Murray, then it would be me. He took it in turns to eyeball every one of us.'

People who spent time with John all agree that his short fuse became an almost non existent fuse when behind the wheel as Martin recalls: 'Me, Ste Birch and Craig Lyon still talk about John a lot. He was just a proper character. You don't meet many people like John Chisnall. He was mad behind the wheel. He suffered from terrible road rage. He was well known for having arguments with other drivers.'

Gary recalls the transport arrangements vividly: 'He had an old white transit van, there were holes under the arch and we would be sat in the back with our coats and hats on going to Blackpool. We'd all be singing. The club later got a grant and Chissy managed to get a Toyota which we all called the "Chissymobile". We used to joke with him about the robot "Johnny Five is alive" out of *Short Circuit*.'

Craig agrees: 'He would take us on the minibus to Blackpool for boxing shows and would be turning round shouting at us if we were messing about. He was always taking the wrong directions too then blaming somebody else.'

Another common theme amongst John's fighters and fellow coaches was his focus on fighters making the weight.

Tony Clarey recalls: 'John was very strict with his rules on boxing and you had to toe the line. He was an absolute stickler for making the weight. If he had a fighter lined up for a fight and the week before he was a pound over the weight, John would go ape. Some of the lads couldn't take it and sometimes even I would think he was going a little bit over the top. Looking back though, if you want to breed champions that's what you have to do. You have to lay down the law and I think that applies in any sport.

'If you look at coaches who have been champions in sport, they have always been strict and down the line. They haven't been soft in any way and that's what John was like.'

Martin puts it in even stronger terms: 'I can tell you what John was obsessed with; the scales. Boxing revolves around what weight you are. He was obsessed with checking our weight. If your weight wasn't right, he would be in a mood and wouldn't talk to you. He would let you know he was upset with you. If your weight was right, he was your best mate. We were new to dieting so if our weight was right, we would go home thinking we could eat a bit more. We'd eat a bit more then think 'what if he checks my weight before we train?' We would lace on all our bandages and get our boots on thinking he wouldn't get us on the scales if we were strapped up to train. Not a chance. He would do surprise weigh-ins and tell us to take our gloves and bandages off. He would even come round to fighters' houses to get them on the scales.'

Gary also remembers the lengths John would go to if a fighter wasn't making the weight: 'As for that, I've only just started drinking water now! I'm a professional fighter, I've won the British title but back then if you put three pound on, he would hit the roof. He lived by the scales. Birchy was that bit older than me and he would be going out clubbing it and so on. John would be going mad at him calling him an idiot for putting four pounds on. We'd go to Birchy's flat in Peasley Cross and John would be shouting up at us. He'd be getting the neighbours to buzz him through the security door, he'd then be banging on the door to get him out of bed and get him down to the gym.'

John's very fiery temper was common knowledge as Tony recalls: 'He upset a lot of people; he was that kind of person. He was the type of man though that if he had anything to say to you he would say it straight to your face. He never pulled any punches on anything. If you fell out with him, it was a long road back.'

Martin agrees: 'He treated everyone the same, he didn't care who you were, you always knew where you stood with him. If he liked you, he liked you, if he didn't, he didn't but at least you knew.'

Gary recalls: 'Nobody would say boo to him, he had a very fiery temper on him but he was respected. He was somebody who didn't give a damn. He didn't mince his words, if you didn't like it, tough. He was a handful. If he said something was red, it was red. He would never beat around the bush. He didn't care who he upset either. To be fair, most of the time he was right.'

Brother Eric feels that there was a change in John's personality in later years: 'John did mellow in later life and wasn't as fiery or hot headed. I think that comes to us all when we get that bit older. We all start to think about things a bit more clearly.'

There was a lighter side to John's character too as Tony remembers: 'We also had some laughs as well. We went down to London once for the ABAs, and we had the likes of Gary Davies and Martin Murray with us. They had the weigh in on a Friday morning. Gary was due to fight on the Saturday. He made the weight then John took him for a big mixed grill. He would have needed a week to work it off. I was saying: "you can't be getting him that" but John insisted it would do him the world of good as it would get "a bit of carbs" in him. "Carbs?" I said. "God almighty, you'll put about half a stone on him."

'One time we went down to London and I just expected us to travel back after the show. John announced that he had booked us all into the YMCA. He said we were going to stay over as we might have a show the next day. I pointed out that it would have been a good idea to let us know as we had families and so on. What a dive the YM was. We were all getting bitten by fleas. There were ten of us in two rooms. I don't think we slept a wink that night. I look back and laugh about it though. We had some great times.'

Sean Casey recalls other trips: 'We had a couple of trips to Germany with the boxing club. We went to Kitzingen near Munich. The German lad who was going to be fighting Wayne was well regarded and they had high hopes for him over there. Wayne always had a big appetite; two nights before the fight they put a meal on for us. I think John had his suspicions about this meal in that they were trying to bulk us up. Wayne must have had three beef burgers this night and John was furious, he absolutely railroaded him. In John's eyes, he had succumbed; he had obviously warned him beforehand about this sort of thing. Wayne, being Wayne, couldn't help himself. That was John though, he was so switched on and dedicated to his sport that sometimes he couldn't understand when other people didn't appear as dedicated and tuned into it as he was. It turned out Wayne won the fight anyway.

'John saw the talent in Wayne and if he could have made it, it would have been a story and a half. John also channelled his efforts and energies into other fighters. He's had a great success with them and had been a massive influence and inspiration for loads of young fighters.'

The local scene was light years away from glamorous boxing venues such as Caesars Palace, Las Vegas as Tony Clarey points out: 'We put on a show where St Helens Town football club played. It wasn't great. The three judges were sat on the stage and we had to put buckets around them to collect water from the dripping roof.'

When asked for any funny moments involving John, Martin Murray makes a mobile phone call to friend Ste Birch. From Martin's laughing it is clear there are some great memories, although possibly not ones suited for publication.

John's devotion to his fighters was unfailing and is something Martin Murray remembers as inspiring: 'We would be around his house for quarter to six every morning; he would get us all in the van to take us training and would do this every day. It was his life.'

Gary agrees: 'I always remember it was me, Martin and Birchy who were the best lads in the gym and were boxing for England. Craig had left the gym at this point. We were training every day, sometimes twice a day. He would have us running around Taylor Park lake in the winter. We'd be breathing out fog in the cold and he'd be stood there like Kojak with his hat on watching us. He loved it, he never asked for a penny more; as long as you paid your subs you were alright. Wherever we went, he paid for everything. He'd be taking us to boxing shows in Blackpool or Wales and we never paid for anything. As a 14-year-old lad you don't think about who's paying for things. Looking back, I wonder how he managed it.'

This devotion and commitment shown to the young men was there to stop them going down the wrong path in life as his fighters admit. Martin Murray reveals: 'When I got to 17 or so, things changed for me. I started going out and drinking and at that age it's like a whole new world, isn't it? Boxing went on the backburner a bit for me then. When I went through the spell of not going to the gym when I was 17, if I saw him in Fingerpost I would hide from him.

'John was disappointed that I wasn't doing it and I then

got involved in trouble. John managed to grab a hold of me and say: "What are you doing?" He got me back in the gym and sorted me out. Something from the past came back up; it was always that with me. However, when I was training with John I never got into any trouble. It was only when I was out of the gym. You usually find that with boxing gyms and with many other sports. He definitely saved me and plenty of others. He completely changed my life and I am doing now what John taught me. If it wasn't for him I wouldn't be doing it. He stopped me from getting into trouble by getting me down the gym.'

Gary also has similar recollections: 'I used to be a handful as a kid growing up. If it wasn't for John I believe I'd be in jail now. If someone had an argument with me, I would batter them. I wouldn't think of the consequences of going to court and getting sent down. John really was my father figure growing up. I went to the gym from being about 11 to being around 19.'

His fighters shared many proud amateur achievements with John, Buller recalls one highlight: 'Chissy took us all down to Wembley for the ABAs. John was proud when Martin won there, so would be very proud of what he is doing today.'

Gary remembers: 'My best moment with John was when I won the England schoolboys title around 1998. That meant I was the best in the country in my weight that year. I represented my country twice that year and won twice.'

There was even the brief prospect of another generation of the Chisnall family entering the boxing world as Eric remembers: 'My grandson wanted to have a little go at boxing and my wife Elaine was not keen. John was very encouraging as you can imagine. He went down and started doing the training. One week, they got his head guard on and put him in a little sparring session with a kid who had been going for a while. My grandson flattened him and

John's eyes lit up. He never went again though; I don't think he wanted to hurt anyone.'

Sadly, the Bobbies Lane gym was to close as the land was sold for redevelopment. Tony Clarey remembers: 'It was a tragedy in itself. I believe the land that it was on should never have been sold for housing. It should have always been for sports and recreation. All the rugby lads and football lads used to train there; it was a community for everyone. I packed in when it closed.'

Tony points out that the closure of the gym meant more than the loss of bricks and mortar: 'Without the gym, it was inevitable that lads would start drifting away and getting into trouble. When you had a community like that that was so close knit you become like parents to the kids you are training. They were able to use boxing as an outlet for their frustrations then they started getting into the sport. They started learning more and becoming good. You get them to that level and they are only going one way and that's up. When the gym closed, that close knit family got broken up. It's like parents breaking up, it's devastating for kids. John would take the lads to Smarty's by The Dragon. He would take them from there down to Huyton to mix with the Huyton lads. He just never gave up. He was in bad health at the time too.'

John's health was now fading as cancer took a hold of him, yet he still gave his all to boxing and his fighters as Tony explains: 'He was invited to go to Uzbekistan as an assistant to the England coaching staff. He did so and had a heart attack whilst he was out there. He shouldn't have even travelled, but he did. That's how dedicated he was to the sport; I don't think he ever recovered from that. He went on a steady decline from that day on. I remember visiting him in Whiston Hospital and he didn't look well at all. I thought he needed to pack it in, chill out and live the rest of his days in a little bit of comfort. It was seven days a week with John.

It probably killed him in the end.'

Gary recalls John's final fight, the fight with his fading health: 'He lost a hell of a lot of weight due to the cancer. I don't remember him like that, I remember him as the man who used to train me.'

Seeing such a tough, strong man as John ravaged with cancer was desperately sad for all those close to him as friend Buller recalls: 'I was with Johnny for 20 years with the boxing. He'd been ill with it for a long time. I used to go and see him at the house. He fought it like bloody hell.'

John's fight with cancer ended in August 2005 when he passed away at the age of 68.

The body gave out; the spirit never did.

Martin recalls the sadness he felt at John's passing: 'John was like a father figure to me. Me and John were really, really close. Unfortunately, when he died, I was in prison and I was really upset. I had been speaking to him all the time and I knew he was ill. I wanted to be there for him and I couldn't. Not being able to attend his funeral is one of my biggest regrets to this day. Hundreds and hundreds turned out for it though, it was massive. The number of people who turned out that day shows the respect with which he was held. Boxing was his life and he helped so many young fighters. He lived and breathed boxing.'

Eric recalls how John's death was a big factor in Martin Murray's life: 'Martin was in prison at the time and couldn't get out to the funeral. I think that hurt Martin pretty badly. Later he said in the paper that he realised he needed to turn his life around when he heard that John had died. So some good comes out of bad doesn't it? It was great watching Martin Murray fight and draw against Felix Sturm for the world middleweight title in November 2011 and it was great for the town and the club. To see him with the Saints badge on his shorts and to hear the crowd singing "Oh when the Saints" was fantastic. He was a half decent little scrum half when he was a kid. He's had a few knockbacks but he's come good in the end. It takes a lot of guts and a lot of hard work to get where he is.'

When asked to describe John's legacy, the tributes come thick and fast. Tony Clarey feels that whilst St Helens will never see another John Chisnall it needs to see another Bobbies Lane gym: 'If somebody asked me to describe John, I'd say, in a nutshell you either loved him or you hated him. Simple as that. John was well known in boxing circles. Not many people involved in boxing in the UK didn't know him. He was passionate about it.

'He will always be remembered as a well respected boxing coach in boxing circles and if you go and speak to old coaches in the Liverpool and Manchester areas they will all vouch for that.

'Certain things I agreed with, certain things I didn't agree with but I respected him as a good boxing coach. As he got older, I would do a lot of the physical work in training whilst John would do the match making and so on.

'He was a tough trainer and never gave the lads a minute but look at the champions he has produced over the years. John was renowned for it. It would have gone on like that but unfortunately, St Helens isn't turning out any boxers now.

'Kids in St Helens need things like that gym. Martin Murray has brought boxing back to St Helens with his reputation and you'll get a lot of kids saying they want to be like him. That's how it happens but you need a base. The likes of me and John were fully committed to it.'

Martin recalls the impact John has on him to this day: 'Even now that he is no longer with us, I still talk to John all the time. Even now, I want to do well for him. As much as I want to do it for my family, I want to do it for him as well. I want to make him proud of me. I saw his wife Carol the other day and she was made up at how I am doing.

'I mentioned John on Sky after winning the British title. My aim as a professional was to win a British title so I could dedicate it to John. It was something I wanted to do and when I finally got the chance, it meant a lot to me. I was made up I could finally do it for him.

'He did a lot for everyone and the number of fighters he produced was incredible. To be a coach and do what they do, it is a full time job. Your heart has got to be into it. If one of us got beat, it would affect John. He was a cracking bloke; I can't speak highly enough of him.'

Gary Davies agrees: 'I wouldn't be where I am in the boxing world if it wasn't for John. A lot of people didn't like him because he said things how they were. At the end of the day, you did it his way or no way at all. He trained me as hard as I do now as a pro. When Liverpool fighters were drawn against any of the lads from John's gym, they knew they were in for a fight. Chissy had us so fit, we used to train six days a week. If we put two pound on we would hear "you're a dickhead". At the same time, he would give you a cuddle if you were feeling down. I never had a dad growing up and John was like a father to me. I've always had a message to John on my shorts in my fights; it says "RIP JC" and I will always wear it. His wife was fantastic too and was always there for him. Carol was a lovely woman. She must have had so much patience as he was always either with us or arranging fights and so on. Behind every good man, there's a good woman and she must have been his. His son Darren was good too; he would always help out at the gym. There wasn't many like John. I still miss him to this day.

'Without John, I would never have been British champion. I would have packed it in a long time ago.'

Craig Lyon simply says: 'All his fighters miss him.'

Fittingly, the final word on John goes to brother Eric: 'He had a massive influence on a lot of young boxers in St Helens. It's one of the hardest games to be in too. It's just you in the ring with another guy and if you don't look after yourself, you get a bit of a thumping. You only get so many second chances. That's the problem with some lads in rugby, you keep telling them things but if they won't listen, they won't listen. You see players who people say can't be reached and you think "I'll be able to sort them out". It happens once in a blue moon that you get to them. It's up to them and whether they want to listen at the end of the day. That's the same in any sport.

'When lads are between 17 and 20, it's a hard time and they think they know everything. If you lose them at that stage in life, you've lost them forever. That's what makes what John managed to do even more special. He turned around kids from all walks in life, some of whom hadn't had the best start in life. He treated every one of them the same.'

10

The Academy Tours of Oz

Whilst John was developing a generation of talented boxers, Eric was concentrating on providing St Helens with a conveyor belt of local talent that would prove the envy of the Rugby League world. It wasn't easy to begin with: 'I used to do a lot with the local schools. I coached the under 16s teams for local schools from 1983 all the way through to the Academy starting in 1996 and on to the present day. When we first started, it could be a real struggle to get kids as the amateur teams would get hold of them. The amateur sides just didn't want their kids playing for our Academy side or Colts. The first two years of the Academy were absolutely diabolical.'

Some of the players they did get would sometimes cause issues: 'Jason Roach came through our Colts system. We were playing a game at Scholes Lane and Jason was having a really good game. He scored a try; afterwards we were looking round for him and saw that we only had 12 players on the pitch. Jason had taken himself off and was lying down on the side of the pitch. "I'm tired, I can't go back on," he insisted. We slung him back on.

'One of the lively characters in the Academy side early on was John McAtee. He was a rum lad. We played at Castleford one day. The referee gave us a caning in the first half; he was giving us nothing. Just across the corridor from our changing room was the referee's changing room. At half time, McAtee took it upon himself to get hold of the key and lock the referee in. We all went out for the second half unaware that the referee couldn't get out.'

The fledgling Colts turned Academy system did start to prove dividends: 'I started Saints Academy side. I got Steve Prescott to play for us in the Academy. I knew his dad Eric. Steve had played a little bit for the Hare and Hounds. There were other good players who didn't make it such as Peter Cannon, a Warrington scrum half who was just a little bit unlucky. It's not always about who is the best player at 16 and 17, they've got to keep improving and developing beyond that point.

'Early on in the Academy, Kieron Cunningham's uncle Gareth was playing for us. Kieron would come down training with us but would then disappear off to Wigan or Widnes. Widnes had lost a lot of their money at that time and couldn't really afford to sign players; Wigan didn't want Kieron because they had signed the England juniors' hooker. Leigh didn't want to sign him either. He came back to us and the story goes that Saints director Tom Ellard offered him £250 and he took it. The rest is history; an amazing career for Kieron and now a bronze statue of him in the town.

'It was the same sort of thing with Adrian Morley who used to turn up at Academy training at Saints as his brother, Chris, was at the club at the time. He was a lanky lad who we liked the look of but Doug Laughton swooped in and signed him for Leeds. We could have had Adrian as easy as pie. You can't get everybody though.

'I remember when Sky started broadcasting Academy games on a Monday night fronted by Graham Beacroft. He was a football fella but he would come round to us before the games asking us about players and what we thought. He tried to get involved and I think he went round to every team that had an Academy. At the time, we would sometimes struggle for players as we were having wars with BARLA over players. BARLA were telling players that if they played Academy they couldn't go back and play in their competition. In the first season of the Academy, we had to go and knock on people's doors. Ray French would give us names of lads and we would go to their houses to try and get them to come down to the club. One name we were given lived at the back of the town hall, we went to see him and he told us that he had never played rugby before but he would come and give it a go if we wanted.

'I did that for two years but then in director Tom Ellard's wisdom he said he wanted me to do something different. I was put in charge of all the youth development at the club; however I believe that was only a smokescreen to get Eric Hughes into the club and get shut of Mike McClennan. Within six months, Eric was head coach.

'The third year, the touch paper was lit and everybody wanted to be involved. Eric Hughes became Academy coach then and they signed about twelve professional players. It must have cost Saints an absolute fortune. I hadn't been getting paid; we just did it for the love of it. When I was in charge, it was costing me around £100 a match. When Hughes took over, he was on about £100 a match.'

Changes were to take place on a global scale as Eric recalls: 'The game became Super League and changed to a summer sport in 1996 after a battle Down Under between television companies over the broadcast rights to Rugby League. I think before the change, the sport had been on the decline slightly. It needed something to reignite everything and I think summer rugby is a fairly good idea.'

1996 brought Aussie coach Shaun McRae to the club. Not only did he deliver a Super League and Challenge Cup double but impressed Eric in other ways: 'The likes of Shaun McRae would often come and do a bit of coaching with the juniors if we had a tough game coming up. He never turned us down and would come and spend an hour with us each time. He couldn't do enough for you; he just loved his rugby whether that be at the highest or lowest levels of the game.'

There were off the field changes at the club as Eric explains: 'I used to do youth development in some of the schools but I was working full time. It needed someone from a teaching background. David Howes, Saints Chief Executive, at the time, brought Nick Halifihi to Saints and that's when things got started.'

Towards the end of the decade, Eric's loyal decades of service at the club were recognised as he was bestowed the highest honour possible: 'I was inducted into the St Helens RLFC Hall of Fame. It was a great night as you don't get to see people from one year to the next. Everybody turns up for these occasions. Billy Benyon inducted me, I have been really good friends with him for many years. Who'd ever think when you sign on at 20 that all those years later you would be inducted into the club's Hall of Fame with players that you were brought up watching and thought of as greats? People like Vollenhoven, Vinty and Murphy. Absolute legends, not to mention older ones who I hadn't seen play such as Alf Ellaby, but whose statistics you saw and what they did for the club. Being part of that is unbelievable.'

Nights such as the Hall of Fame inductions or the annual Past Players dinners not only serve as an opportunity to honour great players and allow former team mates to catch up, they also showcase some Saints' players other talents as Eric explains: 'They would always get Douggie Greenall up singing *Mammy* which was his favourite song. He was a real character. I had the good fortune to go out with him quite a few times. I would go to Lions reunion do's with him and would have a few drinks afterwards back in St Helens. One year, we ended up back in an Indian restaurant in the town with Douggie insisting he be given a steak.

'When I was younger, about 18, I used to go to the Talbot in St Helens; Douggie used to have that pub, his mother used to run it for him. I went in once and asked for a Guinness, his mum told me: "You can't have that Guinness, it's not for sale". I pointed out the crate of Guinness I could see to be told: "That's for Douggie."

'Douggie would do really well in the modern game; he'd play about two games a year and spend the rest suspended. The supporters used to sing "give 'em Mammy" and some opponents thought this was a code name for a plaster cast under his sleeve. It was just his stiff arm though.

'He used to tell the tale of the first time he went to Australia and his reputation went before him. All the journalists were over there asking for Douggie, this hatchet man, this tackling machine. They were disappointed when they saw Douggie, 13 stone wet through. He put that right when he levelled three of their players in the first match.'

Such memories of great characters and legends such as Greenall are part of a club's rich character and history. Looking forward though, Shaun McRae would be replaced as head coach at the club by Rugby League legend Ellery Hanley who was appointed for the 1999 season. Eric recalls it was a turbulent period at the club despite them beating Bradford in the Grand Final: 'There were problems off the field at the club during Ellery Hanley's time as coach and that was all to do with a couple of directors. If I didn't know better, I would have suspected those directors were trying to run the club into the ground. What Ellery did bring us was a ruthless streak. Where we used to be a soft touch in playing the game very honestly, he introduced holding down in the tackle to us and putting a hand on the ball. However, Ellery just thought he was there for the first team and nothing else. I used to run the under 16s town team and the stadium manager kept on telling us that we couldn't train at the ground as it was too bad even if the surface seemed fine.

One night, this happened and I saw Ellery heading out to the car park. I said to him that we were trying to get the lads through the system and we kept getting knocked back. He just said that was nothing to do with him. I told him that sooner or later it would have something to do with him. Come the start of the next season, they fired him off. He was only interested in the first team.'

Ellery was let go after just one game of the 2000 season following a series of public spats with the club's board. He was succeeded by the often controversial Ian Millward. Eric recalls: 'I didn't have much to do with Ian Millward but he didn't have the greatest of reputations inside the club with how he dealt with people.'

In 1999, there were other new faces in terms of junior development with Mike Rush and Derek Traynor coming on board; men who would take junior development at the club to another level.

Traynor remembers an initial wariness from Eric towards the newcomers: 'Eric was probably a bit sceptical of us when we first came. He'd seen a few people come and go who were looking to move on and use it as a stepping stone. I think we proved that we were here to help the lads. That's all Eric has ever been interested in.'

Rush agrees although he had first met Eric seven years earlier: 'I encountered Eric back in 1992 when he coached me as a schoolboy. I was very lucky as Eric and Ian Davies asked me to captain the St Helens town schoolboys under 16s team. That side had the likes of Gareth Cunningham, Ste Barrow and Andy Craig. We had a good side. Young Kieron Cunningham even played for us, a year above himself. Once you leave school, you go your separate ways. I went to Australia, came back and Eric was still here at the club. He was doing what was then an Academy role. He, Billy App, Bobby Dagnall and Steve Leonard or Leo as he is known, got that going. He was running the under 16s side and was probably a little bit disgruntled at the time. I think other people had come into the club and were getting paid for doing Academy roles.

'At first, Chissy was hard to break down. He was reluctant to trust anybody after what had gone on beforehand. He's all about developing young kids for Saints and he wouldn't do it for any other club. I bet he was suspicious when people like me walked through the door. There's only four of them left from the day I walked through the door; Eric, Derek Traynor, Paul and Eric Frodsham.'

Eric admits he took a while to be won over: 'I think you are always wary of new people when they come to a club, so I was when Mike Rush arrived. The first time I encountered him coaching was at Edge Hill when I was on one side of the field with Saints under 16s and he was on the other side overseeing Wigan under 16s. When Nick Halafihi left Saints and they brought Mike into the club I have to say it is one of the best signings the club has ever made. It takes a lot of things to make a good club. Mike has turned the club around completely and the youth development side of the club speaks for itself. Saints are good at youth development because they have it organised. He loves it when St Helens lads come through. A lot of the schoolboy coaches we have in our service areas also serve as scouts. When it comes to signing young talent, if you're in the race you've got a chance of winning it.

'Derek Traynor is a top class coach, he's good with the kids and his heart and soul is with the club. Everybody is who works as part of Mike's team though; if you cut them in half they would be St Helens through and through. They all put a hell of a lot of work in. We all get on with each other too. They tell me if I see anything during training I can have a quiet word with players as we go along. I offer players a bit of advice here and there; whether they take it is up to them.'

Come 2001 and Eric nearly added yet another string to an already impressive bow as Great Britain coach David Waite had plans on involving him in a change to the national structure: 'He was going to introduce Great Britain selectors as they have in Australia. There were going to be four: me, Alex Murphy, David Topliss and Paul Dixon. He got me to send a CV into the RFL but the idea never got passed by the council. Waite did a good job; he turned things around and got some systems in place.'

Back at St Helens and Mike Rush was about to launch a whole new factor in junior development at the club which would have a knock-on effect on Eric's relationship with him as Mike reveals: 'Probably a big turning point with Eric was when we told him we would like to bring him as a VIP on our first Academy tour to Australia in 2004. That broke down an awful lot of barriers and we had also gained his trust from the five years leading up to that. The point when he really let us into his inner sanctum though was on that tour. Chissy is remarkably easy to go on tour with. Our perception pre 2004 was that we were bricking it because we thought he might be a grumpy sod plus he's a legend. Pre 2004 and that first trip, we didn't ask him to fundraise with us, we did it as a collective. Even getting on the plane in truth we were all nervous of going as we still hadn't broken Chissy down completely. Post 2004, the first training session back he said: "Are we going again?" He was full of ideas. He was very unassuming though and we used him while we were away for man of the match awards and so on.'

The first tour was unexpectedly eventful as Mike remembers: 'We played a school; all their kids were on the sideline and we didn't have touch judges. You just don't expect it but 10 minutes into the second half, it was just like a bloodbath. There were players being kicked with some of our lads ending up with stitches in the head. Chissy and Dave Woods ended up on the pitch. It galvanised our lads for the next game really. We played Penrith and they had Michael Jennings playing and we were really fired up.'

Eric recalls the brawl: 'We played Shipley College on one tour. I was sat with Derek Traynor and Dave Woods who used to be the York coach. Dave's our bus driver when we go over. During the game, a fight broke out and there was mayhem. Dave Woods headed on to the pitch so I told Derek we best get down there too. There were speckies fighting; it was murder. Penrith can be quite a physical place though.'

There were also some fun moments as Eric remembers: 'On the first tour we went in canoes over to some bays. Me and Mike Rush had a motorboat, we didn't canoe down. We threw water at the lads and splashed them. They got us out of the boats and walked us round to the top of a cliff. You're meant to jump in the water from the top. I jumped in. I didn't do it again. My feet ended up in the mud at the bottom.'

Saints first teamer Paul Clough recalls the moment when fearless Eric jumped in where others feared to tread: 'We went to go rockpool diving on the tour, all us young lads raced up there but when we saw how high up it was nobody wanted to go. This big shadow came from behind us bombing along and went straight off without even looking; it was Eric. No fear from Chissy and I'm sure that's how he played as well.'

Mike Rush has a different, more colourful recollection of the incident: 'In 2004, he was one of the first to jump off the cliff. He landed with his legs out totally on his arse which was like a blood orange.'

Clough remembers: 'I always remember Eric on the Academy tour as being a very good mentor. He was always full of advice and sort of a father figure. He'd take you to one side and give you something to work on in your game. He was always trying to get you to add little things. He was the oldest guy on the tour and also because of the player that he was, everybody would look up to him.'

Eric recalls another tour activity: 'We took the lads on the Sydney Harbour Bridge climb on that first tour in 2004. It was an experience. I'm not bothered by heights but a couple of the players were; however, they went on and did it. They overcame their fears and were made up that they had done it. We always time it so it's just starting to go dark when we begin the climb. When the players get to the top and look round, the lights of the Harbour are just starting to come on.'

2006 saw the Saints senior side, now coached by Daniel Anderson, sweep all before them as they claimed the Challenge Cup, the Minor Premiership and the Super League trophy before defeating the Brisbane Broncos in the following year's World Club Challenge. Eric recalls a fantastic period in the club's history: 'Saints had become the dominant force in the game in 1996 and went on a period of success for about 10 years or so. They bought the right players at the right times, signing the likes of Newlove then later Long and Sculthorpe. Everything seemed to dovetail into becoming a top class team. Once you do get that team together you only have to keep on bringing in one or two players a year.

'Bringing in Jamie Lyon was fantastic and when he went home, I thought we would never see his like again but he was replaced by Matt Gidley who was just as good.'

Eric feels that the dominance Saints showed in 2006 was partly due to coach Daniel Anderson: 'He was the best man manager we have ever had at St Helens. He was top class, to the point he would go over the top a little bit at times as he used to be involved with everything. We played an Academy final at Leeds once and Daniel came to the match. He ended up sending messages on to the field during the game. He even bollocked them at half time. He is a brilliant fella.'

Shortly after Saints' Grand Final success in 2006, the new batch of Academy players were to tour Australia once again. Eric recalls one current first teamer making an impression on the tour: 'Gary Wheeler is an outstanding kid, he's just been a bit unfortunate with his injuries. If he does get a run though, he will be something special. The second time we went to Australia in 2006, Gary was on the tour. The first game we played was a curtain raiser before Great Britain versus Australia at Newcastle. They targeted Gary as they knew he was a top player. He was hit with a fantastic tackle towards the end of the first half. He was out for the count and they thought he had ruptured his spleen. I had to take him to hospital in Newcastle. We were there for about six hours but he was ok in the end. He didn't miss any games and carried on to finish the tour.'

Mike Rush recalls the incident: 'The first person to offer to take Gary Wheeler to the hospital in Newcastle was Chissy. He sat with Gary a long time until we could come and pick them up. Eric even rang Gary's family on the way to the hospital to let them know he was alright.'

Saints star Jonny Lomax also went on that 2006 tour and remembers Eric's influence: 'Eric was great on the Australian tour I went on. Sometimes, some of the coaches might blow up at us at half time as coaches do. Eric would just have a quiet word with us before we went back out on to the field. He would speak to you without all the emotion of what was going on in the game. He would give me a bit of advice and tell us to keep doing what we were doing. He was so helpful and was always filling us with confidence.'

The third Saints Academy tour of Australia took place in 2009. Eric recalls a familiar face made an appearance: 'Daniel Anderson had just returned home after completing his contract at Saints. We turned up at Balmain for a match and there was a knock on the door shortly before kick off. It was Daniel. He said he just wanted to come in and say hello to us all. We drew the game after a couple of bad decisions. In the dressing room after the game, our lads were singing *Oh when the saints* as they do after games. Daniel came in and was in the middle of it singing along with them. At the final game of that tour, he turned up again when we played at St Mary's in Penrith. After the game, as is his way, he was holding court with all our players and coaches.'

Another current first teamer made the 2009 tour as Eric remembers: 'Tommy Makinson has come on leaps and bounds. He really has worked hard for it too. Before we went to Australia in 2009, I thought that what let him down perhaps was his lack of speed. We did lots of sprint work before the tour and I believe he carried that on himself, doing sprint after sprint. He has improved and has put three or four yards of pace on. He ended up being one of our best players on that tour. He actually won us the last game against Penrith. They made a break and one of their lads was heading for the line. Never-say-die Tommy sprinted after him and caught him. He is a dedicated lad, he started off as a centre and I think that's where he will end up. He can learn his trade on the wing first, that's what the Australians do.'

Mike Rush feels Eric had an important influence on Makinson: 'He was very close to Tommy Makinson in Australia. The making of Tommy was Australia. He was like a Tommy gun in the way he wouldn't stop asking questions. He was a little bit of a nosy kid in that he'd want to know what we would be doing on a Wednesday when it was Monday. Chissy had a little word with him after day two.'

Saints junior player Marcus Baines recalls: 'I went on the 2009 tour with Eric. He was the member of coaching staff who if you had any problems, like homesickness, you would go to. He's the mentor of the group. You respect him when he talks because of everything he has done and everything he carries on doing as well. When he made porridge on tour, he would be putting milk in when the other coaches would be using water.'

Fellow junior tourist, Adam Barber, also praised Eric's porridge making skills: 'He does a mean porridge. He was really encouraging on the tour. If you'd had a bad day he would be the one to have a chat to you. He would advise you on what you needed to improve.'

Star Jonny Lomax laughs when asked about Eric's famous porridge but says: 'I never tried his porridge because I didn't like it at that age but he made a mean beans and scrambled egg on toast. I can vouch for that, it was very good.'

Mike Rush has the final word: 'Eric mucks in with everybody else and he's brilliant at making porridge. For 21 days on tour, he makes porridge every morning. '

Mike also recalls that Cronulla in 2009 was the scene of Saints' only defeat in their four tours: 'We have only lost one game on all four tours; we got stitched up a little bit because we believed a certain friend of ours, that he was fielding a certain 'weakened' side at Cronulla. That turned out not to be the case. We still could have won that game. We bombed a few chances, and at one stage I thought we were going to win easily.'

2009 also saw a momentous occasion in Dave's life as he was inducted into Warrington's Hall of Fame. He also led out the Warrington cup final team of 1975 onto the Wembley turf prior to the 2009 Challenge Cup Final and received a rapturous ovation from the Warrington fans.

2010 saw a momentous time in the history of the St Helens club as the iconic Knowsley Road ground would open its doors to the public of St Helens for the last time after the club announced plans to build a new stadium. Eric recalls with sadness the passing of the 'old lady': 'I felt sad when Saints left Knowsley Road in 2010. It was done for economic reasons. I can understand that because they couldn't get grants to redevelop Knowsley Road. That was the top and bottom of it and the ground had been neglected for a long time. I think the last time they had done anything was when they built the executive boxes in the late 80s. It was just a little add on rather than rebuilding; same sort of thing when they did the restaurant in the 70s. It wasn't any good in the end. We loved it though; fantastic playing surface, a place speckies used to love to go to. All the people from Eccleston and Thatto Heath would walk down there. I spent from 1966 to 2010 there; it's a life. Actually, my involvement with the ground started before that when I used to go watching the team as a kid. During the last season at Knowsley Road, we had a Past Players Dinner out on the famous turf. We all had our pictures taken.'

Coach of the senior side in that last season at the ground was Mick Potter. Eric says: 'Mick Potter was a nice fella but a bit quiet and only really comfortable with the rugby. I think he's a bit of a shy person. He came on one of our Academy tours watching the games but he didn't get as involved as Daniel. He's a bit more laid back.'

2010 saw serious illness once again afflict the Chisnall family. Les recalls: 'I had a stroke in 2010 and it's hard to recall things sometimes now.'

Dave was also seriously ill: 'I had a lung removed because of cancer. I was shocked when I was told I had cancer. It was devastating and frightening.'

Eric recalls the amazingly quick turnaround of Dave leaving hospital: 'He's retired now and has suffered from ill health. He had cancer and had to have a lung out. He went into Broad Green Hospital to have it done and within a week he was out.'

2011 was a season with a difference for Saints; whilst their new stadium was being built, they would spend a season out of town, playing in Widnes. The team suffered a horrendous run of injuries which Eric saw as a blessing in disguise: 'It brought youth into the team, which in turn brought enthusiasm and lifted everybody else.'

The club was further rocked by the news that two of its England internationals would not be renewing their contracts at season's end as Eric recalls: 'It was announced that both James Graham and Kyle Eastmond would be leaving the club. With James, he didn't get any stick from the crowd as he just put his head down and got on with it. Kyle was a bit immature; he had only just got into the first team really and hadn't fully settled into his place. He's a little bit naive and worries a bit too much about everything. If he does something wrong, he thinks about it for ages and ages. I remember one of the Grand Finals we lost against Leeds, Kyle hadn't played well and was sat on his own at the hooter. I went over to talk with him. He's just a deep thinker. He told me his mum says the same thing about him in that he sits on his own and thinks about things. He just needed to learn to let go and just play. I talked to him once or twice during the 2011 season and told him to just get on with it. He told me that the crowd were all on his back. I explained that all it would take was two or three tries from him and the crowd would forget everything they had been saying about him. I think it was best not playing him at times though as it wasn't good for our club. I don't think it should ever happen where supporters should ridicule one of their own players even if you might not like him. No player ever goes out on to the pitch and doesn't try his best. It may not be good enough but it's the best he's got on that day. Maybe he didn't help himself by doing daft things to the crowd. Once Kyle gets something in his mind though, he's dead stubborn.'

During the season, Saints would achieve a remarkable feat in their match away to Harlequins as Eric proudly declares: 'When Saints played and beat Harlequins away in 2011, there were 12 of the team that had been on these Australian trips with me. The 17 itself contained no overseas players. That's the aim of it all. I know you can never get 17 local lads in the team, you've always got to have imports but the idea is to get as many local lads in as you possibly can. You need a good scouting system which Derek Traynor looks after and is absolutely fantastic. Then there's all the coaching that goes on and people who volunteer their time and energy to make sure the kids are progressing. We want to get all the best kids in St Helens, the odd one out of Wigan and Oldham. We've currently got one from Barrow so you have to be looking everywhere.'

In his after match interview following the Harlequins victory coach Royce Simmons was quoted in the St Helens Star as saying: 'The players can be very proud of that as can the club and the town of St Helens. It's thanks to the likes of Mike Rush, Ian Talbot, Derek Traynor, Ste Leonard and all the volunteers that we can do this.'

Prior to Eric accompanying the players on a fourth Academy tour of Australia at the end of the season, a celebration dinner was held to celebrate Eric's 40 years at the club and to raise money to pay for the tour. Eric smiles as he remembers: 'It was a surprise event for me but my wife Elaine was involved in it. I thought I was going to a Union/ League fundraising night. I went to the Indian in Rainhill on the Friday night and a friend said, "Are you going to Greenalls tomorrow for that do?" I told him I was going to one at Ruskin Drive. I mentioned this to Elaine when I got home and she told me she had forgotten to tell me that they had changed the venue. I never twigged though. It was a fundraising event for the 2011 Australian Academy trip that took a look back at my 40 years at Saints with all the young players who I'd brought through. There were about 160 kids that I'd coached over the years who were there. It was a really good night; there were people like Mark Lee and Bernard Dwyer who I had coached very early on.'

Steve Leonard credits the turnout with Eric's standing

amongst those fortunate enough to know him well: 'The testimony is the number of kids who turned up for the dinner we had for him. He was mobbed by players from every age group. That's the person he is.'

Eric credits head coach Royce Simmons on his actions before the party left for the 2011 tour: 'Royce was made up with the youth set up. If I asked him to do anything with the juniors, he would do it. Before the 2011 tour, all the players were being presented with their jerseys and because of injury Conor Dwyer was going to miss out. Royce still presented him with a shirt and gave a nice speech about him. That went a long way with Conor.'

Eric outlines the format of the ultra successful tours: 'Each tour lasts for three weeks. They've all been really good. I'm not being funny but when I went away with England as a player, you just did what you wanted. There was no structure to the tour. On these Academy tours, everything is organised and disciplined. The tours are all about playing rugby and no other reason. There's no boozing which includes all the coaching staff as we need to set the example for the kids to follow. The players are all aged 16 or 17. They go as boys and come back as men. You get to judge them in different environments and how they react when they're out of their comfort zone. We stay at Narrabeen, a sporting school of excellence for athletics and swimming; Manly Sea Eagles also train there. We stay there for the first four days in dormitories. We then travel up to Penrith and stay at a complex right near their Leagues Club. It's just like a wooden shed with rows of beds, similar to an army barracks; seven beds three high. We do our own cooking and feed the lads as best we can. Sometimes they go out and have meals; it's such a fantastic trip for them.'

Mike Rush recalls some of the memories of the most recent tour in 2011: 'We were lucky because we had both Eric and Tommy Martyn. Tommy shared a room with Eric.

Eric helped out with the shopping and the cooking. We've been away for over 100 days across the four tours and he still joins in every activity.

'In 2011 at the age of 65 he still took part in the white water rafting. Poor old Tommy Martyn had come out of his boat and one of the lads went across to help him but Chissy decided to hit him on the head with his paddle. He made him go all the way down on his own; he wouldn't let him in his boat and just kept hitting him with his paddle. We sometimes worry about his age with such activities as white water rafting but if everybody else is doing it, so is Chissy.'

Eric remembers the rafting: 'Like a big fool, I did some white water rafting whilst away with the tour. We did it on the Olympic slalom course at Penrith. I was just watching at first and remarked, "that looks easy" so they said I could have a go. I only came out once which wasn't so bad.'

Junior player Jack Jones remembers that moment well: 'He came out of the boat and I recall seeing his head bob up and down.'

Steve Leonard recalls Eric as the immovable object: 'The guides were trying to get us all out of our boats during the white water rafting but Chissy took some shifting.'

Former coach Daniel Anderson would be a frequent visitor to Saints' 2011 tour as Eric remembers: 'First week, he turned up. He's doing media work in Sydney now after his sacking from Parramatta. He had a cup of tea and a bit of dinner with us. What you might not know is that his claim to fame is being able to wrap stuff up in clingfilm. We'd be wrapping butties up for the lads and he'd be shaking his head and would end up taking over. He travelled an hour and a half to watch us in the Cronulla game. He dropped his wife off and brought his two kids over to watch it with us. He then came to the final game at Penrith. I feel he has a real soft spot for the club. I think if the timing is right and they ask him, he will come back to St Helens. I asked him outright and he said: "Never say never." Maybe he misses it. I think coaching is different in Australia as the sport is more high profile and the media give people a bit of a bashing. In England, he only had good things said about him.'

Mike Rush recalls some of the humorous moments from the tour: 'It was a snore off between Chissy and Gordon Pennington. Even on the fourth tour, I asked Chissy to room with us but he stayed with the masses. He's never got out of the mess yet. He originally got moved in there because of his terrible snoring. Anybody new goes in the mess like Tommy Martyn and Killer (Neil Kilshaw). Eric has four tours in and still hasn't got out of the dorm. I think he enjoys Eric Frodsham's company when we're away. They always end up cooking and cleaning together.'

Eric recalls rooming with former Saints star Martyn: 'Tommy was always up first thing in a morning and out; he couldn't sleep. I would switch off if I woke up, turn over and have another half hour.'

Mike Rush outlines some of the laughs the younger players unintentionally provided: 'We were all in canoes on Sydney Harbour when one of the kids asked, "When do the activities start?" He was in a canoe in one of the most picturesque locations possible. Eric has never gone in the canoes; he's always joined me in a speedboat. He had a go at surfing though on the first trip, the second trip when we tried it I think he went for a coffee with Leo.'

One such trip with Leo ended in embarrassment as Eric remembers: 'The players would go to Bondi to do some surfing. Me and Leo would ask to be dropped off by Eastern Suburbs club because when I had been over with Saints in 1976 I had stayed around the corner from there. We had had all our meals round there so it was interesting to go back and have a look. Me and Leo had our dinner there. Dave Woods came and picked us up and mentioned he had been talking to the owner of a local club. He had told her we might be dropping in to have a look. He took us there and told us to knock on the door telling her Woodsy had sent us. A woman came to the door and we explained we had come for a look round so she took us through. We sat on a settee in a lounge area, then a couple of scantily clad ladies walked in. At this point, me and Leo were more or less holding hands. We made our excuses and left sharpish. We didn't half give Woodsy some stick over it.'

Rush explains just how involved Eric is on the tours: 'Chissy mucks in with all the chores on tour and has had a group of kids on every tour. Even when his kids aren't at breakfast, he is still there. Notoriously, I am always last up, as Leo puts it, "I sleep more than the *Blue Peter* tortoise". Because I now have three kids and am more used to getting up these days, I would surprise Eric by being up and he would often ask, "Have you shit the bed?"

'Eric used to mother the likes of Jordan Case and would let him get away with only eating half his porridge at breakfast time.'

Junior player Brad Ashurst recalls: 'I went on the 2011 tour with Eric. He's a top bloke and he's always there to put his arm round you. He's always willing to show you the ropes. He's definitely on the side of the players. Chissy is probably the person I would go to the most before a game. He's been there and done it, hasn't he? He's just Chis, isn't he? He gives good advice.'

His thoughts are echoed by player Jack Jones: 'He's a top bloke and you can speak to him about anything. When I was there, I felt a bit homesick and I went to him straight away. Then I would talk to him about rugby and he'd tell you what needed to be done. He's always straight with you. We all look up to him with all the appearances he has made for Saints. He's a legend. I'd have a chat with him often in the social room on the tour.'

Steve Leonard details some of the banter that occurs on

the tours: 'We have told the kids that the last time Eric toured Australia he did it by boat. We were up the Centrepoint tower in Sydney and we could see one of the old, tall ships coming into the harbour. I told some of the kids that it was the same boat that had brought Eric to Australia. They were like "is it?" I advised them that they were better asking him than me. I got out of the way sharpish. He's still got a grip on him. He grabs me in jest only it's round the neck.

'The tours get the kids used to dealing with adults. Beforehand the only adults they have ever really had to deal with have been family and teachers. We're not regimental but we get our point across.

'One of my highlights of the trips is when all the kids have gone asleep on the plane. I can't really sleep when I'm flying and Chissy only cat naps. We end up having a couple of beers stood at the back.'

Eric confirms the story: 'Me and Leo have a stroll to the back of the plane, have a beer and a put the world to rights session on our trips to Australia. Leo's another one who is doing a fantastic job. He also helps with the Players Association now.'

Mike Rush gives another insight into the 20-hour flight to Australia: 'One year I offered to share business class with Chissy. After about 10 hours, I went through to swap places but he was asleep so I thought I'd better not disturb him and went back to business class! It backfired on me though because on the way back, I hadn't slept a wink and all the lads in coach came skipping off the plane in Dubai after a 10-hour sleep. I was gutted.'

Eric, laughing, disagrees: 'He's a bloody liar, he never came down. I always sleep with one eye open. Us old 'uns are tough anyway, we don't need business class.'

Eric uses the tours as part of the education process of younger players that he himself once went through: 'On the most recent tour, we took the team to watch the Test match between Australia and New Zealand and I was advising the lads to watch Thaiday running off Lockyer closely. I used to watch good players and if something that they did worked I would try and incorporate it into my game. Timing is everything when you are learning your trade; when you are putting moves on you need to be able to hit the ball with pace. I learnt it when I came to Saints. Graham Rees, the old Swinton forward, was a master at timing. We'd be putting moves on and he would physically grab hold of my jersey just as I would be ready to set off. He'd hold me back until it was the right time for me to go.'

The 2011 tour saw the young Saints unbeaten again which leads Eric to question why the national side fails at senior level: 'In that tour, we again didn't lose a game and we defended like I had never seen us defend before. I never thought we could defend like it, they were magnificent. Our record is just the one loss in four tours. I just can't understand where it's all going wrong when the players go into first grade? Why can't the England team compete against Australia at senior level when the same players are able to do so when they are younger? On our tour, we played Penrith, their best team, and Cronulla who finished in the top four of their Academy league. We are not going over there and playing ham and eggers. I can't put my finger on it but there's something missing somewhere. Maybe we are bringing too many imports into our game. I found it concerning that Heighington and Chase were picked for England in the 2011 Four Nations tournament when in my view they are no better than what we've got. To me, Rangi Chase is a New Zealander. End of story. I think we need to dig deep and bring our own players through.

'One of the problems for England is that through bringing in so many imports, we perhaps lose some home grown players. I think we also sometimes discard players at too early an age. There's a belief that if a player hasn't made it by the time he's 20 then he's never going to make it, but there's always late developers. I don't think that the 20s competition is a top competition. I think it needs to be revamped and thought about seriously. We just seem to dabble at things; there doesn't seem to be a set structure and direction in which the game in this country is heading.

'Saints and Leeds have contested four of the last six Grand Finals; they are the two clubs who have done most in terms of developing young English players. Everybody else seems to be after the quick fix, they don't want to work hard. I think if clubs came out and explained to spectators that they were trying to build a team long term then the speckies would be behind them.'

As to why other clubs haven't followed Saints in developing their own Academy tours to Australia, Eric is blunt: 'I can only answer "nobody's got any brains". Others have tried it but have made a right horlicks out of it. We go, taking 29 kids plus staff. The staff do exactly the same as the kids, we train with them and cook with them, we are one big team. Of a night, the staff don't go down to the club boozing. I've heard certain clubs treat such trips as a piss up. We stick together doing the same thing and we are one unit. I believe that really does hold the tour together. I remember remarking on the first Academy tour, "I came here for 13 weeks with Great Britain and I didn't do half the stuff these lads have done". Everything was organised for them and nobody was left to their own devices.'

Steve Leonard agrees that the tours have a definite focus: 'We keep the trips relaxed with things building up to game day. The lads know when to have a laugh, when to go to bed and when to switch on for the game.'

Mike Rush details what it has taken to conduct the four tours: 'It consumes your life for the two years you have to raise that money. We've had to raise in total around £314,000 now. It's a massive commitment for your family. I've got three young kids, Derek's got two grandchildren, Leo's got three grandchildren, Killer's got a little lad with another one on the way. The pound is weaker against the dollar which has made it harder. We did it though and we will keep doing it. It is tough, but we've involved Chissy by doing a dinner for him. He didn't get any money out of it but he appreciated it. We enjoyed doing it and we made a couple of grand for something that is close to Chissy's heart. There's only Derek, myself and Chissy who have done every single tour.'

The tours have paid clear dividends as Mike Rush reveals: 'There's a culture of talking about rugby in this place, it's not just your job, it's your hobby. There's nobody who doesn't put silly hours in. We have great volunteers and all our full time staff do two jobs as opposed to one. People say to me: "It's alright for you; your kids get a trip to Australia." I feel like saying, "yeah, who do you think does all the fundraising?" We work to make it happen then we get the success off the back of it. We put money into the club by holding fundraising functions at the club's facilities. Some junior players are attracted to come to the club because of these tours, they come because culturally, educationally and rugby wise this is the best place to be. It's like if you're picking a school for your child, you send them to the best school. This is the best place for kids to come to if you want them to become rugby players.'

Mike and his team's dedication to youth development for St Helens shines through in every word: 'We've never had designs on becoming Super League head coaches although I helped out Daniel Anderson in 2008. I only did so on the understanding that I would come straight back to what I love. (Mike was also appointed Interim Head Coach for the bulk of the 2012 season prior to the appointment of Nathan Brown). We will probably get 30 years out of bringing the kids through. Not everybody can be Sir Alex Ferguson but

Chissy has had 46 years by sticking to something that he knows. Other people he knows like Frankie Barrow, and even his brother Dave, have coached and it doesn't always work out.'

11

Cowley

Early 2012 and house music pumps away in the gym as Mike Rush jokingly asks if they have stopped playing S Club 7 in there. Chissy says: 'It's good music this' with a beaming smile across his face.

St Helens RLFC's training facility at Cowley is a place where champions are made. The love and dedication of Mike and his team shines through; not just in the hours that they put in but their approach and the way they speak to the players. There is a whole culture there, a culture of respect. In a room full of typical teenagers at a sports club, you would expect swearing yet it very rarely happens (they were heard discussing Facebook). One gets a friendly tap on the back of the head as a gentle reminder that he shouldn't be sat with his leg over the side of a chair.

A poster on the gym door contains the Lou Holtz quote: 'The answer to three questions will determine your success or failure. 1 – Can people trust me to do my best? 2 – Am I committed to the task at hand? 3 – Do I care about other people and show it? If the answers to all three questions are yes, there is no way you can fail'. This ethos can not only be applied to a sports team such as St Helens but to any small business and even parenting. Every age group uses the facility from the under 13s, to the first team. That culture of respect and the club mentality of St Helens are ingrained in them. It's a very healthy, positive culture. It's not military style; it's done with all the best intentions for those boys in mind. You can see the satisfaction Mike and his team get from developing those young men as players and as people, developing them further than perhaps the players themselves felt they could go. Eric Chisnall is a big part of that.

From the 3G pitch where the players run through drills with great energy and ferocity to a hyperbaric feature, an outstanding gym and a massage room; everything is designed to get the best out of the players.

Junior player Marcus Baines outlines Eric's involvement and approach: 'At 8 o' clock on a Saturday morning, he is here at Cowley. While we are moaning, he has a smile on his face.'

Eric acknowledges the hours he puts in and his wife Elaine's approach: 'With my work and my time I spend at Saints, I have to say that my wife is very understanding. She gets on to me now and again, saying I do too much. After a day at work though, I have a headache. Your mind is switched on all day, organising jobs, quoting jobs and so on. I come home, put my Saints training kit on, head to the Cowley training facility and the headache disappears. I just love it, it's my safety valve. Sometimes, it does get a little busy. I'm there for three hours on a Tuesday night, same again on a Thursday night; I'm there Friday nights and on a Saturday too. If it's a match day, that means I'm there a little bit longer. I'm still very keen on watching the first team too.'

Eric can also clearly state from experience how lucky the modern players are to have the fantastic Cowley facility: 'The training facilities, barring the gym, have been the same for players at Knowsley Road for the past 30 years. At Cowley, the players have everything: a magnificent gym, split levels with running and rowing machines upstairs. It's open to the Academy, the 20s and the first team. Obviously, the equipment at Cowley is fantastic such as the oxygen chamber and the ice bath although I don't think I would ever have fancied a dip in that myself. It's how times move on though. The younger players asked me how I managed without weights. I told them I was working and lifting steel all day which made me strong. The game has changed in simple ways, like we never used to be allowed water during a game; we were told it would give us a stitch. We played in 100 degree temperatures at Wembley in 1976 and they wouldn't give us a drink of water.

"Killer' (Neil Kilshaw) is so well educated on the sports science side of things; they know what they are doing on the fitness and technical side. They know how to build training and what to be doing during the pre season. The preparation of the side is second to none. The players are expected to keep the gym tidy too; we have to keep on at the kids all the time about that. If the first team comes in the gym the next day and it's a mess, they go mad. It's all about discipline, once you have that in your game, you are halfway there.'

Steve Leonard confirms Eric's approach to discipline: 'Eric doesn't believe in players cutting any corners as he believes they will get caught out, so he likes to see if they are cutting any corners in the gym. You're not going to pull the wool over his eyes; he's been around too long. If he notices it, he will have a quiet word with them and tell them that it will catch up with them. They've got to be honest with themselves first, then honest with the coaching staff. He doesn't miss a trick but he won't slag a player, he will go and tell them.'

Mike Rush outlines how Eric's values form a big part of the culture at Cowley: 'Eric puts in countless number of hours at the club. Chissy is generally the last person out of the gym after a training session.

'He helps us raise money to take the kids to Australia and does it for nothing. All the guys in our team do; there's Precky and Glyn. We have Eric as one of the assistant coaches for the under 18s, we use him as the good guy. We have to hit the kids often enough with the harsh realities of "that wasn't good enough" or "this isn't up to standard". They see Chissy as a bit of an uncle, he doesn't have to stand in the changing rooms and say "you're not picked". He can step back from that and say "that's ok, don't worry about it". He can draw on his own experiences so he still does that. He has an input into the team and he also has an input into discipline. When we go on tour, he is one of three people who are on our disciplinary panel. Four tours and we've never had to use it.

'He's got a lot of good friends at the club through the four trips he has been on. We see him every week, a couple of times a week no matter the weather.

'Before the trips to Australia, the coaches were viewed as just coaches. Since the trips, they have really built real relationships. As we are all about developing young kids, once they have flown the nest up to first team we are here for an arm around their shoulder, but they don't get any more bollockings from us. We have to remind them about tidying up after themselves on the odd occasion but nobody ever answers us back. The players see Chissy and the other coaches as respectful figures who did a lot for them. We also have that with the kids who don't make it, as we point out to them that it might not be through a lack of effort or lack of ability, it might just be through lack of luck. That's why the father figures we have created at the club are so important. There are plenty of kids who hold him close to their hearts. He can give that love to them because there were times when he went through not getting picked. You'd have to go a long way to find someone who doesn't have a good word to say about Chissy.

'We have a strong ethos; we don't let the kids swear much. Eric loves the club and we encourage the kids to try and spend time with him and ask him about his playing career. The kids have seen videos of him playing as we have shown them to them but they take the piss because they are in black and white. We try and prompt them to ask him about National Service.

'I'd like to think Eric loves every minute of being down here with us and that he loves everybody's company here. He told me that the tours we have done were more enjoyable than the ones he did as a player as they never did the activities that we do. We are there not only to develop young players but to develop young men. Not many of our kids have come back and ended up going down the wrong path in life or being disrespectful kids. A lot of them grow up really quick, we give them so much that it makes them grow up and it makes them see people in a different light. You ask them to do something but there are rewards at the end of it. It forms discipline.

'We've generated men of steel in James Graham and James Roby; we've won Super Leagues, we've won Challenge Cups; the driving force for me and Eric now is to get as many St Helens kids into the side as possible.'

Those men of steel are quick to praise Eric's influence, James Graham remembers: 'The first time I met Eric was at a St Helens schoolboy team match. I'm pretty sure it was under 13s. He was someone I immediately respected and looked up to, which was some achievement with me being a rebellious teen. I remember the look he would give us if we swore. The discipline he instilled in sides he was involved with was excellent and something I still remember even now, and something I'm very grateful for. There were many times when I was starting to step out of line and he was always there to guide me on the straight and narrow.

'Being a forward definitely helped too. He always had good tips about carrying the ball and looking for support. Thinking about it I was very fortunate that I was under Eric's guidance as a youngster. There are many things that he helped me with that I still use today.

'As I moved up into the first team he was someone I would still see around the club with the youth teams and Academy set up. He always asked how I was going and about how my dad was doing. I hope that he continues to have a role at the club with the young lads coming through. Hopefully he can instil the same values in some of the next generation to wear the red V.'

James Roby agrees: 'Eric coached me when I first came to the club as he was coaching the Academy then. He coached me for a number of years so I've known him quite a long time. He was always a friendly face and always really approachable. He was always there for the lads and I think the lads saw him as the one they could go and speak to, I know I did anyway. He wasn't somebody to be scared of. He would be on the side of the lads and had done it all himself throughout his career. As a coach, I would take note of what he was saying. When you say the name "Chisnall" you associate it with St Helens straight away. Eric is such a nice guy inside rugby and outside it as well. You can speak to him about anything. He was really good for us as a team in the Academy and was always helping us out. It's amazing the amount of hours he put in and indeed still puts in at the club. I wouldn't like to see the total amount of time he has given to the club. When I came through, I started playing half back and maybe a little bit of loose forward. As time went on and I started playing in the forwards a bit more, it was great having someone like Eric who had been a forward himself. He automatically gets respect around the club.'

Coaching the under 18s probably helps keep Eric young even though some aspects of their interests leave him cold: 'I'm not into Facebook or Twitter no matter how much some of the younger lads at the club go on about it. Why does anybody want to know that you've just been for a cup of coffee? I know James Graham once gave Paul Wellens loads of stick at a fans forum for how daft he was on Twitter. I do think players need to be careful when posting things that concern the club. You don't want to be giving out information that helps other teams. You can also say something that you mean as a joke that somebody else can take in a completely different way. Some of the stuff that some fans say on internet message boards also amazes me; some of them don't seem to know much about Rugby League.

'I'm old fashioned, I do have a mobile but I hardly ever text people. I try to ring people usually. I also keep asking the players why they don't bring Max Bygraves in and play that in the gym. Some of the head banging stuff they listen to is bloody awful. They're all doing their slick moves to it but it's not for me.'

Eric is keen to emphasise the benefits to young players of choosing St Helens as their club: 'I would tell any parent looking for a Rugby League club for their son that Saints is the best choice. It's the type of rugby Saints play. Coaches sometimes try and change it but it always shines through. The club also looks after players off the field and develops them as people. Young players are taught through the day and then stay there for training. Saints have got everything in place and everything's right.

'I would never swear in front of the junior sides, when they get to around 18; they might hear me swear a couple of times and the reaction is always the same: "I thought you didn't swear?" We try and instil discipline into the players and that discipline is not just in rugby, it's in your life. It should be in everything that you do, in turn that will make you a more complete player.'

There is no doubt that Cowley will be a draw for stars of the future; to come to Saints to develop themselves as players and as people.

Eric continues to act as a positive influence to current first team stars too as Derek Traynor reveals: 'He is like a father figure to the kids. He has a calming influence and has a quiet word with players. If we've been having a go at them you will see him go and have a little word after and put his arm round them. When Jonny Lomax made his first team debut, he rang Chissy on the way panicking. "I need to speak to Chissy; I need to speak to Chissy". He was asking "what do I do?" He is highly respected by the young lads. He's a smart fella and once you're his friend you would have to do a lot to get him to turn away from you.'

Star half back Lomax remembers: 'I first met Eric when I was 16 going into my first game for the under 18s. I'd been down to one or two training sessions then ended up playing for the foundation Academy. One thing led to another and the next thing I was playing for the under 18s. Eric had been helping me at training and just talking to me. He told me to keep my head and be myself on the pitch. He had a quiet word with me just before kick off and it worked as I ended up scoring a hat trick in my first game. It was good to have him there as he's a massive calming influence. Whenever I see him now I always have a good chat with him. He's very approachable but he's just a nice guy. Eric's always at the club and he's a guy you can just go and chat to.

'Eric had dropped me a text before my first team debut away at Wakefield and I wanted to give him a ring. When I first made my debut I wasn't as close to the likes of Kieron Cunningham as I am now. Obviously Kieron offers me a lot of help now. Chissy was one of the past players, one of the legends, I spoke to him and he calmed me down and told me not to do anything rash on the field and that I should just be myself. It was good.

'One thing you hear a lot as a player is that you should play the percentages. You need to weigh up the options and risk of a particular decision on the field. I remember once, we were a little bit behind in a game and I threw a pass that was intercepted. Anyway, we ended up winning the game.

The coaches were saying I hadn't weighed everything up when throwing the pass. Eric quietly said to me in private, "Jonny, if that pass is on, you throw the pass. They only just managed to get hold of it. They're not calling you if we score from it and that wins us the game there and then. Back in my day, when I was in the pack, they used to get on to me about not throwing the long pass out. I played at Wembley and saw the winger was coming up out wide, I threw a long ball to him and nobody was calling me when he went straight down the wing and scored". That's how Eric used to back up his advice and it's one thing I've never forgotten.'

Eric clearly rates Jonny highly: 'Jonny rang me on his first team debut panicking slightly, asking me: "What do I do?" He's such a nice lad but he's a bloody worrier. He likes everything being right, he doesn't like doing anything wrong. When he plays he likes to give 100 percent. A lot of people, on their debuts, worry about things they don't have to worry about. A lot of the younger ones are put under that much pressure nowadays, they are playing a bit younger, the games a bit faster, there's more hype and the cameras are on them. It is harder to make your debut nowadays. I just told him that once he got on that pitch, he would forget everything else. You just go on automatic pilot where you do the things you've got to do. You concentrate on the things you've practised and the things you are good at. That's all paying dividends for Jonny now. He's going to get better and better.

'Jonny is something special; he has got the heart of a lion. I first met him when he was 16. You could see that he was going to be special. When he came over to Australia with the Academy he was our top player. He's a good, genuine kid who doesn't give any bullshit. He does it and he puts his heart and soul into it. If he does something wrong, he will go home and talk it over with his dad, he'll then be out on the field practising what he did wrong to put it right. I know he has spent a lot of time on his kicking because when they're kids, they don't have to kick so much. 2011 was his first proper season at half back and on occasions, he carried the team through. For a young lad to do that is incredible and he is only going to get better. He still listens and talks to you, and if you say something, he will take it on board. I tell all the Academy players to listen to people offering advice, they should let it go in and if it isn't any good let it go out. If it is useful, keep it in the memory bank. There are all sorts of little bits and pieces that make a great rugby player.

'Saints have a history of scrum halves with tons of personality: from Murphy to Goulding to Long. A scrum half has to be cocky, confident and a little bit bossy. He can't be shy and has to be able to tell people what to do and when to do it. Rumour has it that when first playing for the first team at scrum half, Jonny Lomax wouldn't shout at the other players. James Graham and Leon Pryce told him that until he started shouting at them they would whisper to him. It's difficult though when you're a young lad first coming into a team as you don't want to be too cocky. That can have the opposite effect where established first teamers think you're a little bit too big for your boots. They want more talkers in the game today. When we played, there would be talkers and then doers. The half backs have got to be great communicators now as they've got to drive the bus so to speak.

'It's unbelievable how far Jonny has come in the game already. As a teenager he took a bad knock and had major surgery on his head. It was touch and go but he came back.'

Other young players make Eric proud too: 'Lee Gaskell is one on his own. He's done really well. Mick Potter had a liking for him and due to injuries in the 2011 season he got a lot more games. He's more of an individual player rather than making other people play. If you watch him play, he will do something that nobody else in St Helens Rugby

League club can do. He can just glide past people and never looks like he is struggling. It all just comes instinctively to him. He's just so natural. When Saints defeated Wigan home and away in the 2011 play offs, he was nearly breaking the line three or four times, a bit more confidence and he'd have been through. Everything just comes so easy to him.

'You can tell with certain ones that they're going to make it. The first year, it was Paul Clough. He was so dedicated, he ate, slept and dreamt Rugby League. That's all he wanted to do. He would train at Saints then go and jog home down the East Lancs Road. It's paid off for him. I built Paul a chin up machine for him to work out on at home. It was just a primitive one but he could use it at home. I used to have one myself when I was about 25.'

Clough is another established star quick to pay tribute to Eric: 'He's up there with the all time greats at the club. He played for his country and played for Saints for so many years. He started off young and played for a very long time. Someone like that is very well respected.

'Because he was a forward and because he knew the game, I would speak to him. Also, as well as knowing about players from the past, he would often talk to us about certain players in the NRL. He'd talk to me about Paul Rauhihi and how he had an offload in his game. He said I should look to add things like that to my game, always be improving as it would make me a more complete and therefore better player. What was great about Eric was that he could talk to me as a forward but could also take a half back or a winger to one side and give them advice. He's very versatile in his coaching because of the knowledge that he has.

'Every time I see him, I always go and speak to him because of the respect I have for him. The same goes for Kieron Cunningham and Paul Wellens; he's obviously helped them over the years. They've always got time for him. He's still a good friend and I know I can ring him for advice and he'll always be there. He's a great bloke.'

The St Helens conveyor belt of talent has continually churned out fantastic players and there are more still to come as Eric reveals: 'In our most recent intake, we seem to have a lot of good kids. You might get a year where there are only one or two who can go into the first team. All things being equal, there are quite a few of the latest crop who, if they stay injury free, stay dedicated and keep their feet on the ground, should make it.

'As for who will be the next players to look out for, I'd say Luke Thompson. He's a 6ft 1in second row forward who can catch pigeons. He just needs a bit more nous. Then there's another second row or loose forward, Conor Dwyer, son of Bernard. His problem is that he's just had a bad injury and has had two operations on his leg. I take the mickey out of him about his pace saying, "well at least you're faster than your dad". When I had just finished playing and I was training the Colts we used to go up Scholes Lane playing tick and pass. Bernard made a break and I was just at the back of him letting him run. I let him get to about two yards from the line and I ticked him. He said: "How did you catch me you fat bastard?" "Easy", came my reply.

'James Tilly is another good forward, Danny Yates is a good scrum half, Dom Speakman is another good half back. Then there's Mark Percival at centre who is a bit in the Lee Gaskell mode. If he wants to beat someone he can do it without blinking an eyelid. Some years you might get one or two coming through who make it into the first team, sometimes it's three or four. If you get one a year, great, if you get two, you're laughing. From the group who went on tour in 2009 though, the floodgates have opened for them in terms of opportunities.'

12

Abide with Me

2012 saw a huge moment in the history of St Helens RLFC with the triumphant opening of their fabulous new Langtree Park stadium. An initially sceptical Eric was impressed: 'I was one that didn't want us to leave Knowsley Road but even the pitch at Langtree Park is far superior to the famous old turf we enjoyed at our old home.

'Having been shown around Langtree Park before it opened, it was a different world; seeing is believing and I changed my mind. The new stadium looks good and I think we were very lucky to start building at the right time. From the changing rooms to the corporate hospitality, it is fantastic. I find it difficult to drive down Knowsley Road where the ground used to be. Ironically, my work unit backs on to Saints' new stadium. I was even asked to do some work on the ground but we were too busy at the time.

'Eamonn McManus has done really well for the club. By all accounts, if he hadn't arrived at the club, we'd have been dead and buried. The club had fallen into the wrong hands along the way. Back when I started, we had Mr Cook and Basil Lowe who always had the best interests of the club at heart. You'd have 12 directors with one pulling all the strings who'd have seven or eight others on his side. Joe Pickavance then took over in 1974, later it went to Tom Ellard and Mal Kay.'

The first Super League game at the new stadium saw

Saints take on the Salford City Reds. The club did itself proud with the way they handled the opening of the ground. *Abide with Me* was played as a guard of legends including Eric formed around the tunnel area. South African legend Tom Van Vollenhoven then strode out with the match ball in a classy touch uniting both eras and grounds of the club. For Eric, things had come full circle. The same Tom Van Vollenhoven who had urged Joe Coan to pick a young Eric for the Lancashire Cup Final replay was now alongside Eric, both players' statuses secure as true legends of the club they had served so well.

Eric recalls it as a special night: 'Being part of the guard of honour for the first game at Langtree Park was absolutely fantastic. They played *Abide with Me* which is a rugby song. It's such an emotional song too. It's old fashioned but people still like it. Bringing that to the new stadium along with all those players was a wonderful link between the two grounds, the past and the future of the club. Eamonn McManus is keen for the same people who were involved at Knowsley Road to be involved at Langtree Park. They are welcoming the past players and spreading them about the different corporate areas so they can mix with different sponsors and so on. It brings Knowsley Road to Langtree Park. It keeps the spirit of St Helens Rugby League team going.

'When Tom Van Vollenhoven walked out with the match ball, the hairs stood up on the back of my neck. It made me think back to various memories of the past. It made me think about how great a player Tom was and how great the other legends in the guard of honour were too. It was just the icing on the cake on a historic night for the club. It was well planned and well executed.'

Younger brother Dave had a somewhat different first visit to the ground as Steve Leonard explains: 'Some players leave a club and there is a little bit of ill feeling towards it and I think Dave has that a little bit with Saints. Eric brought him to an event at Langtree Park to try and give the club another chance.'

In a classy touch, Saints had decided to brighten up the stadium concourses with murals of some of their most famous players throughout its history. One such mural features both Eric and Dave. Eric recalls their first look at it: 'The picture of me and Dave at Langtree Park on one of the concourses is absolutely fantastic. It's something that you never think will be done about you. I took my wife, Elaine, and Dave and his wife, Carol, for a look round the stadium and it was funny. When we got there, Eamonn McManus was in reception and came over to us. He had been on the phone to Alex Murphy who had explained he would be a little bit late coming. Dave has played golf against Eamonn so they started talking about that then the talk switched to rugby and Dave said: "Well, I'm a Warrington specky".

'We went round the ground looking at the images, when we came to ours. Dave was absolutely made up with it. I don't think people realise that he played 114 games for Saints. He always wanted to play for Saints and it just didn't work for him at the time. He used to go to Warrington Past Players functions because I think he felt a bit harshly treated during his time at Saints. As time goes on, you do mellow. We had a Past Players evening at Langtree Park and our Dave was there with his mate Ken Kelly. Ken is another one who classes himself as a Warrington player as he never wanted to leave Saints when they sold him to Bradford. They both said to each other that they didn't need to go anywhere else now as they both felt welcome again at Saints. That's what's happening now; we are getting former players coming back to the club. It's not Past Players anymore; it's the Players' Association, as we are getting younger players joining too.'

Whilst the new stadium was a welcome and much needed development, Eric has concerns about how the town itself has shaped up in recent years: 'I'd say that over the past four or five years St Helens, as a town, has changed beyond all recognition. It's sad to say it but I think it's going to the dogs. I walk into the town centre and it is empty with shops closing. It's full of people trying to sell you bits of bric a brac on the streets and pound shops. You go to the other end of town and see drug addicts hovering about on the streets. Westfield Street used to have all kinds of independently owned little shops, now it's full of bars. I know the council is trying to blow the trumpet over the new stadium and the bridge and that's great but it doesn't make a town does it? There are a lot more other people in St Helens than those just interested in the rugby.'

As for Saints themselves, Eric sees a common theme across the years: 'The ability to win games late on is something that has stuck with the side into the modern era. You can easily recall numerous occasions in Super League when Sean Long has done it in the dying moments for Saints. We have also generally always played entertaining rugby league. The names of the players change but the spirit does not. I think we've been lucky that we've stuck to our guns in those respects and have had the quality of player to keep it going. Various coaches have tried to change us; Mike McClennan tried to change us a little bit in the early 90s. With each coach though, rugby always came to the fore. Somehow or other, we have always been the team of class who would play a bit of football. We've always signed that certain type of player as well. Each coach has tried to change us, it's never worked and thank God it's not. If we went to become a boring style of team, I don't think we would get the spectators we get. I think St Helens spectators stay to the end because they still think we can win it at the end.'

Eric was further encouraged when Saints travelled to Widnes in the 2012 Challenge Cup and the debut of Adam Swift meant the line up that day included products from each of Saints' youth tours to Australia in 2004, 2006, 2009 and 2011.

In December 2012, Saints forward and graduate of the youth system, Shaun Magennis, was sadly forced to retire prematurely due to injury and paid tribute to Eric amongst others: 'I'd like to thank the fans for their support and the coaches I have worked with. Eric Chisnall, Derek Traynor and Mike Rush all put a lot of faith in me. I'd also like to thank my family for being there.'

Eric has strong opinions on today's game in general: 'It's just so different now and the mindset has changed in that some players train for 20 minute spells. I just can't understand that. There are a couple of props who look to play for the full 80 minutes such as James Graham and Jamie Peacock. Then there is James Roby who plays the full 80 week in week out. I know the few times in my career that I was on the bench, it was very hard to come on and get used to the pace of the game.

'The game today is different, some elements for the better, some not so. Doing away with the head high tackles has improved the game. Players are a lot fitter these days because they're full time professionals. I'm not certain about skills; some of the players from years ago were very, very skilful. As kids, they played with tennis balls and bits of paper taped up. At school, we would be playing silly, little games with balls. They all developed skills though. There was no television so we were out playing all the time. We'd be playing tick and pass for three or four hours at a time.

'There is a lot of coaching going into the kids today and there are some good players. The one thing I cannot stand today is the standard of refereeing. They've not cottoned on to the idea that if you let a player go offside by an inch, the next time he'll go a yard. If you let him pass forward, he will do it again. Rules are there to be broken and referees are there to stop you. Today's referees just seem to sway one way and then the other. They try and even things up and make a game of it instead of calling it down the middle. They concentrate too much on keeping the penalty count even whether it deserves to be or not. That's not the important thing; it's where on the pitch you give the penalty and what number on the tackle count you give it.

'The game today is fast and tough. I'm not 100 per cent happy with Sky; they make the rules up as they go along and seem to change their mind about things all the time. A classic example is when they talk about the momentum rule; if you throw a ball forward it's forward. I don't think that Eddie Hemmings really understands Rugby League. He's learnt the rules but not the finer subtleties of the game.'

Dave shares Eric's concerns about the sport today: 'I don't think there's as much bullying goes on in the game these days, stuff like putting people off their game. It was win at all costs when I played and I do think that the game has gone soft.

'We weren't on contract money like players are today, if you lost it was tough then you had all the missing wages if you were off work from being injured. My grandson is 17 and plays rugby union for Liverpool St Helens. His dad used to play Union too. He's 6ft 1in and has that aggressive streak. He gets told off by the referee a bit, I don't know where he gets that from! He loves his rugby. I'd sooner go watching my grandson play Union than watch Rugby League, there's a bit more bite in it. However, the profile of Rugby League players is better now though than it was back when I played.'

He admits to having a soft spot for Warrington: 'I still get on well with the Warrington supporters to this day. I've always found them tremendous, they know the game. I still go and watch Warrington play from time to time although I don't go as much as I used to.'

Ken Kelly outlines the reception Dave receives when

visiting Warrington: 'He's a legend to this day. We go to a few games now and then and the Warrington supporters are shouting his name. They love him there. He appreciates them in return and thinks they're a great bunch.'

Prior to the start of the 2012 season, Dave was invited down to Warrington to present rising star Chris Hill with his shirt for the campaign.

Health wise, whilst Dave is now suffering from Alzheimer's which has affected his memory, he takes great pride in his four children: Phil, Michelle, Jeannette and eldest son Lee who now lives in Perth: 'We've been over to see him a couple of times and he's doing well for himself.'

Typically, for the Chisnall family, despite Dave's achievements he remains modest: 'I've done alright but I don't really brag about myself.'

Friend Ken Kelly tells a story that typifies Dave's attitude: 'We were at John Bevan's testimonial match down at Tylerstown in South Wales. We were only in a village and had played on a mountainside. It was called "heart attack hill". The day was absolutely red hot too. After the game we went out into this village. We were all on the beer then. The next thing, Dave was in the street talking to these Welsh fellas. Dave then comes running into the pub, out of breath. I asked him what was wrong and he said he had just had a set to with a couple of these "Welsh bastards" as he put it. This big bloke comes in asking Dave what the hell he was doing flattening his mate. Dave said: "he should have learnt to button his mouth after talking about us coming down here". The bloke said: "You shouldn't be here anyway". Dave said: "We're here for John Bevan". "Oh right," said the bloke, "come on Dave, I'll buy you a pint". He had come in to fill him in and ended up buying him a beer. That's how Dave was; he would talk his way out of anything. He's a character. They threw the mould away with him.'

Brother Les has sadly been unable to work for the last 20

years after a devastating road accident. You can tell from talking to him that his heart is still at Knowsley Road in some ways as he recalls: 'Saints was always my favourite ground to play. '

As for modern Rugby League, Les's view is: 'I don't enjoy some aspects of the game today although I do have to say the players are fitter.'

Looking back at his long and illustrious playing career, Eric reflects on some of his favourite moments and places: 'My favourite places to play were always Leeds and Swinton. I liked Swinton because my first final was there and I scored a try. I always seemed to play well there. The first time I went to Leeds I ended up scoring a 60 yard try. They kicked the ball; Ken Williams caught it and passed it to me. I just started running; I went past a couple of people and ended up scoring by the side of the posts. Again, every time I went to Leeds I seemed to do ok. Leeds were a decent footballing side as well. It wasn't just battles all the time with them.

'The Wembley matches would have to be the favourite ones of my career: 1972 Wembley, you always remember your first. The 1976 Wembley final was the real icing on the cake though. My first Lancashire Cup Final also stands out. The first Championship Final in 1970, I thought I did really well in that one.'

Eric's outlook on life and society today is undoubtedly influenced by his tough childhood on Havelock Street: 'I do think that with younger people in general today that everything comes too easy for them. It's just modern life. If younger people don't work today, their mums and dads look after them, give them money and buy them cars. They are spoilt. I had bugger all growing up and it still affects my outlook today. Elaine will talk about us buying something and my instant reply is, "we can't afford it" even though we can. I'm murder really. I've come from being on my uppers to doing okay for myself. Some of it is being in the right place at the right time and being lucky with rugby and with my work. I've worked two jobs and I've worked hard. Now I try and look after it for my wife, kids and my grandkids.'

Eric believes in treating people the right way, something he saw in other Saints players throughout his career: 'I remember one local man used to come into Saints and he was down on his luck. Every time Bob Dagnall would spot him and give him a few quid and he would turn to us and say: "There but for the grace of God go I". It's nice to be nice to people.'

Eric reflects on his two rugby playing brothers: 'Me, Dave and Les are the only three brothers to win at Wembley. A few pairs of brothers have won but we are the only three. It is an achievement in itself.

'The three of us don't get together very often really. It's just one of those things, you just drift apart. When my mam was still alive, every Saturday we used to go round to her house. The house would be full with the grandkids and so on. We should make a bit more of an effort. I went to my grandson's christening in 2011, our Les couldn't go but Dave was there. He's not in the best of health and it made me feel I should make more of an effort. He's had cancer and his memory isn't as good as it was.

'The name "Chisnall" is synonomous with Rugby League. It's something we've earned. We've worked hard for it, all of us, in particular my mother who brought us all up on a shoestring. Our mum instilled a lot of the grit and fire that we all have. We say things as they are, we are honest and we don't call people behind their back.'

Whilst John excelled as a boxer and then as an outstanding coach and mentor of young talent, the three Rugby League Chisnalls are the only three brothers from the same family to win the Challenge Cup, also uniquely they each won it with a different club.

Today, the very name 'Chisnall' evokes memories of

sporting excellence and leaves a lasting legacy amongst the young sportsmen who the brothers have personally inspired and coached.

With boxing champions dedicating their title wins to the Chisnall name and international Rugby League stars still picking up the phone for advice, the Chisnall legacy shines as bright as ever.

The name will live on.

Fittingly, the final words go to those who know the Chisnalls best.

Kiwi coach Mike McClennan says: 'St Helens is one of the loveliest places on this planet, the people are marvellous. They gave me a bit of stick early on when we weren't enjoying the best of success. They deserved and needed success. I loved my time there.

'The first thing you get off Eric is a big smile. I can only give him every accolade as a man. I know he was a tough footballer too. He held his spot for a long time in first grade at the mighty St Helens club. I would go into the Alder Hey club and Eric would always come over with a big smile and shake my hand. I would think "it doesn't come any better than this". He's a lovely man. He really is a standout and I met such wonderful people in St Helens. He's right at the top.

'The Chisnall family are so valuable to society as sports people and more importantly, as people. They don't come any better. What a great family they are.'

Rugby League legend Alex Murphy says: 'It's amazing that three brothers can come out of one family and all play rugby and also have another brother who was a boxer. They were all ruled by their mother who was probably tougher than them all.'

Mike Rush says: 'We worked out that Chissy has done 46 years at Saints as a player and a coach. He's a lovely bloke and he's a St Helens lad through and through.

'His decision to go to Leigh was probably made in haste and probably made in regret. I'm sure he would have loved to have been a one club man. It wasn't to be and the good thing was that he ended up back at Saints.

'Now, we feel like we've known him all our lives after him being initially nervous to open up to us. With his upbringing in Havelock Street as one of many kids, losing his dad quite young means that he fights for everything he gets. He's a really honest hard working fella. He doesn't suffer fools gladly though.

'He has done it all for the right reasons. I'm sure there were times when he didn't want to come to the club because of a couple of personalities he may not have liked. It's obviously close to his heart for him to persist and keep doing that. He did the schools, the Colts and the Academy then people came in and started getting paid for that work. He clashed with a couple of directors too. If he wasn't so passionate about what he does, he had plenty of excuses to walk away.'

Saints junior player Dom Speakman says simply: 'Chissy always has words of wisdom for us, he is always telling us to play smart.'

Former team mate Geoff Pimblett says: 'Three aspects of Eric spring to mind straight away: size, pace and football ability! He was a big lad, who could certainly handle the rough stuff. I remember him coming to help me on one occasion when I was getting some rough treatment from the Australian tourists at Knowsley Road. Then there was pace, Eric was a wide runner who would cause opposing defences some real damage with the ball. Thirdly, he was an excellent footballer with good hands. Remember his long passes? He did one at Wembley in 1972 against Leeds and put Les Jones in to score by the corner.

'Eric's defence was also very good indeed, especially his one on one tackles. Mind you, they were great days in the early 1970s, we were a really good side and everyone knew his job on the field. We were a real family club too. Perhaps Eric's real value to the side could be seen in 1978, when he got injured in the first half of the season and ended up missing Wembley. Eddie Cunningham had to move into the second row from the centres and we ended up losing to Leeds. But that's how much we missed him when he wasn't in the side.'

Fellow team mate Billy Benyon says: 'We had a truly great side in the early 1970s and Eric was one of the best back-rowers around at the time. He had all the skills with the ball in his hands. He was quick through the gap and a sure tackler. He was a thinking player and knew the game inside out. He was confident and thoroughly deserved his representative call-ups. The large number of matches he played for the Saints speaks volumes about his commitment to the club too. Team spirit was so good when he had established himself in the side. We were mates on and off the field. There were a lot of local lads in the team, which did help enormously. It's no surprise to me that Eric has continued to be involved at youth level with the Saints and once again, he has done a fantastic job, he has always loved the game.'

Paul Loughlin says: 'He's always been there at the club. The length of time he has spent at the club is a great achievement.'

Sean Casey's take on John's legacy is powerful, 'There's still a picture of John up in Lowe Housing Boxing Club to this day with an inscription from Kevin Bacon, who is a coach now at Lowe House. That reflects the influence that John has had and continues to have. Not just the big names such as Martin Murray but also lads who didn't go on to have boxing careers. Those men still talk about him and have nice things to say about him.

'I would never have gone to the boxing club without John; the grounding it gave me and the attitude towards work and sport that it gave me was key. I will carry them with me for the rest of my life.'

Martin Murray sums up the humour and affection of the family: 'There are so many funny stories about John but it's difficult thinking of one that's clean and can be printed.

'Eric's the same; he's a great bloke too. He was one of those people you could mither and have a laugh and joke with.

'They're a talented family when you look at it with three of them winning the Challenge Cup at Wembley and the fourth becoming a professional boxer.'

The Chisnalls left everything they had out on the pitch or in the middle of the ring. They were successful in their own right but were special enough people to inspire and coach generations of future stars. The following Mary Anne Radmacher quote seems almost written for the way they have approached life and it cannot be denied they have lived its principles to the full.

'Life is all about risks and it requires you to jump. Don't be a person who has to look back and wonder what they would have or could have had … Live with intention. Walk to the edge. Do what you love. Live as if this is all there is.'

Postscript

The morning after the manuscript for this book was finished, Dave Chisnall sadly passed away at his home in St Helens after his battle with cancer. He was 64.

As news of his death spread, and Sky Sports News rightly referred to him as a 'Rugby League legend', tributes and personal anecdotes filled with love and respect flooded social media and internet forums.

A character, a Rugby League force of nature, a gentleman and a family man.

Dave Chisnall, gone but never forgotten.